Managing the Demand for Fashion Items

Research for Business Decisions, No. 73

Richard N. Farmer, Series Editor

Professor of International Business
Indiana University

Other Titles in This Series

Managing the Demand for Fashion Items

by
Rajendra R. Bhat
Manager of Information Analysis
ADP—CES
Hayward, California

UMI RESEARCH PRESS
Ann Arbor, Michigan

Produced and distributed by
UMI Research Press
an imprint of
University Microfilms International
A Xerox Information Resources Company
Ann Arbor, Michigan 48106

Library of Congress Cataloging in Publication Data

Bhat, Rajendra R., 1953-
  Managing the demand for fashion items.

  (Research for business decisions ; no. 73)
  Revision of the author's thesis (Ph.D.—University
of California, Berkeley, 1982).
  Bibliography: p.
  Includes index.
  1. Fashion merchandising. I. Title. II. Series.
HD9940.A2B48   1985   687'.068'8   85-1039
ISBN 0-8357-1618-X (alk. paper)

To My Parents
Ramanath and Prema

Contents

List of Figures

List of Tables

Preface

Traditionally, the retail merchandising of fashion items by an institutional buyer has been considered to be an art unamenable to scientific analysis. The main reason for this has been the lack of knowledge of the demand dynamics for these items. Recent advancements in computer technology have made available the infrastructure for capturing, storing, and maintaining data on the large number of transactions at the retail level. This monograph provides a better understanding of some of the important issues in managing "fashion, nonperishable" items.

Chapter 1 provides background on fashion merchandising management and describes the barriers which have restricted research on this topic. Chapter 2 discusses and classifies some of the important models which have been developed for managing fashion merchandise inventories. The institutional structure for the buying and retailing of fashion items in a large department store is described in chapter 3, where an understanding of how institutional buyers operate, and the strategies they use in the dynamic environment of fashion merchandising is provided. Chapters 4 and 5 discuss the data collection methodology employed in this study, and analyze the actual data. Empirical data on sales, inventory and price of a few fashion garments are used to investigate the demand structure over time. It is shown that the sales to inventory ratio, called "k," can be used to measure the sales performance of a fashion item. Hypotheses on the behavior of "k" are formulated and tested. These hypotheses deal with the important factors that could influence "k," notably time in the season, price, inventory, and special periods such as Christmas. Regression analyses of "k" against these variables give an indication of the magnitude of the effects of these variables on "k." Chapter 6 develops two models: a simple markdown model is formulated that could be used by the fashion merchandising manager to evaluate the economics of a markdown plan; and a control theory model is presented that specifies the optimal price path for a fashion item given the response function for "k." The concluding chapter summarizes the main findings, and also discusses some of the topics which require further study.

The material in this book should be of interest to both academicians and practicing managers in the fashion retailing industry. Students specializing in retailing management would especially benefit from the material presented in chapters 3, 4, and 5. Practicing managers could use the concept of "k" to control their stock of fashion merchandise by a simple process of plotting "k" over time, as shown in the numerous plots in the book. When better computing capabilities are acquired, managers could move toward the decision support framework presented in chapter 6.

I am deeply indebted to Louis P. Bucklin, who originally suggested this topic to me, and was instrumental in obtaining the cooperation of the department store that provided the sales and pricing data for this research. His help and encouragement sustained me during the difficult stages of my work, and his insight and advice have greatly enhanced its quality. Some sections in the introductory and concluding chapters were a result of a working paper that I co-authored with Pete Bucklin.

I would also like to thank James M. Carman, who kindled my interest in the application of management science techniques to marketing problems. I sincerely appreciate his comments and suggestions. Thanks go as well to Andrew W. Shogan for his valuable suggestions. Andy has been a source of inspiration to me — he is a terrific teacher and the perfect role-model of systematization and organization in one's work. I especially want to acknowledge Dr. Lenny Auerbach, Dr. Pirie Hart, and the wonderful staff at Barrows Hall for their help and encouragement.

I would also like to express my gratitude to UMI Research Press for their confidence in my work, and for their very important role in the successful completion of this project.

My wife, Anita, deserves special mention for her love, patience, and understanding during the research and writing of this book. My daughter, Supriya, had the important role of keeping me entertained and busy.

Rajendra R. Bhat

Alameda, California
March 1985

Fashion Retailing and the Decision Sciences

During the past ten to twenty years, fashion has played a much greater role in soft goods merchandising. "Designer" brand names have won increasing patronage; and there has been a noticeable quickening in the pace of style change in merchandise lines long regarded as staple items. Merchants have responded with more frequent promotions and a greater emphasis on advertising and sales events[6]. This is evidenced by a steady increase in the markons taken by fashion merchants and in the ratio of markdowns to sales.

Data from annual statistics published by the National Retail Merchants Association clearly show these patterns. In 1955, markons for department stores in the sample were 38.8%, while markdowns averaged 5.6% across all merchandise categories [13]. In 1980, the figures were 47.6% and 11.1%, respectively [34]. The greater opportunity for gains from a successfully maintained markon and the higher possible losses from markdowns have made the task of successfully buying fashion merchandise more challenging.

Despite the increased risks in the sale of fashion merchandise, fashion buying and merchandising have rarely been studied systematically. Recent texts in retailing suggest that concepts for the development of fashion merchandise budgets have changed little over the years. The exceptions to this limited theoretical development are Cyert, Marsh, and Moore's descriptive (but now aging) model of department store ordering [10], and Pessemier's provocative, but terse monograph on retail assortments [30]. Application of the decision sciences is limited to studies by Wolfe [39] and (more recently) Johnson [19]. The majority of research on retailing has focused on shopping behavior, store image, and location.

A major barrier to the development of theory and improved decision making is the absence of accurate knowledge of the demand for fashion merchandise being sold at the retail level. In particular, little is known about the time path of fashion merchandise after the assortments are placed on display. The key issue of whether sales are stable over the season, build up or diminish, or vary randomly, remains largely unexplored. Is there a comparable pattern across product lines, or do systematic differences exist? What roles do price and the change in seasonal demand play? Does the effectiveness of promotional activity vary over the season? While skilled institutional buyers must intuitively develop an understanding of these questions, there has been little formal investigation of effective management of the demand for, and the inventories of, fashion merchandise at the retail level.

Fashion Inventory Management

The effective and efficient management of inventories is a problem that occurs in all sectors of the economy and in all functional areas of management. The annual investment in inventories in all sectors of the economy runs into billions of dollars; and there is huge potential for increased savings by improving the management of this important asset. A wide disparity prevails in the degree of sophistication of inventory planning and control techniques employed in different sectors of the economy. Typically, manufacturing industries are at the forefront, utilizing sophisticated inventory management techniques in their operations. Retailers, however, still use the "rules of thumb" that they have developed over the years to manage their inventories. There are historical and practical reasons for this state of affairs.

Variance

The variance (or variability) of the demand for an item at the production level is substantially lower than the variance at the retail level. This is generally true when the production facility caters to a number of retail outlets. (For example, if the demand at the retail level is an exponentially distributed random variable, it can be shown that the variance of the sum of a number of these random variables which represents the demand at the production center becomes smaller as the number of terms in the sum decreases.) This regularity in demand at the production level simplifies inventory management. It is easier to build analytical models for inventory planning and control when the demand is steady, or has a low variability. In contrast, the demand at the retail level is highly volatile. The analysis of predicted sales is complicated by the high degree of uncertainty associated with it.

Data Collection

Data collection is easier at the production level since the number of transactions is small and the average number of units per transaction is large. On the other hand, at the retail level there are typically a large number of transactions, and the average number of units per transaction is very small. The tremendous increase in the number of observations leads to data collection problems. These problems are compounded by the geographic dispersion of the outlets in a retail chain operation. Therefore, the cost of data collection is much higher at the retail level.

Willingness to Experiment

There has been a greater enthusiasm for experimentation and acceptance of management science techniques at the production level. Management science and operations research techniques were developed during World War II and were applied in the production area with some success. Production engineers and management scientists "speak the same language," and are thus able to understand each other.

Risk

There is a higher degree of risk at the retail level. Normally, the retailer absorbs the losses when a product does not sell in the market, and there is a high inventory of the product. The producer, on the other hand, is normally protected by explicit contracts that specify the terms and conditions for the supply of the product and any returns that can be made by the retailer.

Other Factors

The impact of economic, sociological, and psychological factors is very highly pronounced at the retail level. These factors are generally not as critical at the production level, which simplifies the modeling of production inventory problems.

In a retail store, there may be a high degree of interaction between the quantity and mode of display of an item, and the sales volume. A customer may normally look at a number of substitute items in a particular category before making a purchase. Therefore, in order to make ordering/pricing decisions for a particular item, the retailer must consider the total picture, including the interaction between different items in a category. The retailer also has a larger repertoire of control variables which can be used to optimize revenues, sales, or other criteria of interest.

Recently, important new developments have necessitated a change in retailers' traditional techniques for inventory management. The cost of computer hardware has been steadily decreasing, and with these changing economics, retailers have installed point-of-sale terminals, high speed data communication equipment, and large scale data storage devices in their businesses. As a result, data collection and storage problems have been greatly reduced. Management scientists are looking at multidimensional marketing and retailing problems. They now have the tools, the techniques, and the data to help them attack and solve the complex problems faced by the retailer. In turn, retailers are becoming more receptive to management science techniques.

Fashion Merchandising: Some Definitions

Before proceeding further, it may be useful to define several terms which we will utilize repeatedly. *Webster's New World Dictionary* defines a "fashion" item as "something, especially a garment, in the current style." Fashion merchandise is subject to systematic, and usually rapid, changes in style and to highly volatile demand. The life cycle of a style is typically short and, depending upon the item, may range from ten to thirty weeks. This period is referred to as the "season." After the end of the season the demand for the item (if any) will be many orders of magnitude below the demand during the season. Nonperishable items are products that can be stored for a long period of time without undergoing any physical changes (i.e., they do not physically deteriorate or degrade over time). Examples of fashion, nonperishable (*F,NP*) items are Christmas cards and fashion garments. The focus of this monograph will be on (*F,NP*) items.

An (*F,NP*) item is typically purchased only for a single season. Retailers make most of their commitments to buy from producers prior to the start of the selling season. Reorders may be attempted for especially successful items, but product availability is typically limited once the season commences. The retailer is usually responsible for the sale of all items purchased, regardless of the price required to clear the market. Returns are a luxury enjoyed at best by retailers with substantial power in the channel.

In brief, the fashion buyer's task consists of two parts: the creation of merchandise assortments to meet expected demand and, in the light of realized demand, the adjustments of remaining assortments by pricing and promotion activities. The first task calls for the selection of the set of fashion items whose present value from anticipated sales maximizes the return on the funds the buyer has to invest in inventory. The second requires the buyer to adjust the rate of stock depletion to maximize the present value of the merchandise on hand. These latter decisions, therefore, are based wholly upon the relationship between the market price and sales. Original cost is "sunk" and irrelevant to maximizing cash flow.

The successful implementation of both of these tasks requires an understanding of the time path of demand over the season. A new fashion item that sells quickly is preferred, other things being equal, to one for which unit demand is similar but develops more slowly. The management of extant inventories similarly relies on this understanding, since initial sales rates provide signals for evaluating how demand will unfold and the types of strategies that may be enacted in order to obtain desired stock. The theory and empirical evidence developed in this monograph will relate solely to this time dimension of demand.

Most of the inventory models in the literature on fashion items are based on assumptions about the nature of demand for such items. Because these assumptions are not supported by hard empirical data, product managers and buyers in the retail trade have largely ignored them. They regard the task of managing their line of fashion items as an art which is not subject to scientific study. Consequently, a large number of "rules of thumb" and norms based on the practical experience, hunches, and beliefs of managers have been developed in the industry.

A scientific study of the nature of demand for fashion items at the retail level is now not only feasible but is essential to the development of mathematical models for inventory planning and control. In the following chapters, a theoretical basis for the structure of retail demand and some basic models for managing fashion inventories will be presented.

2

Classification of Inventory Models

This chapter will develop a classification scheme for items based upon those characteristics which have influenced the development of inventory theory. Some of the models in the literature on inventory planning and control in the retailing industry will then be examined. The focus will be on inventory models that have been developed for fashion, nonperishable (*F,NP*) items. The pricing literature in economics and psychology will also be studied for any relevant insights.

Historical Perspective

There are a number of economically sound reasons for holding inventories, be they physical goods, cash, personnel, or any other useful resource of value. Without inventories, it would not be possible to meet demand at the time of its occurrence, a situation leading to increased costs or lost profits. For example, a retailer might lose customers temporarily or even permanently, if demand were not met immediately. Sometimes, the unsatisfied demand could be met, but at a higher cost. A manufacturing facility might incur idle time for its productive resources if it lacked sufficient raw materials inventory, leading to increased operating costs. Inventories can also be used to take advantage of lower prices for certain seasonal items, or to stock up in anticipation of shortages or a supply breakdown. In certain situations, especially at the retail level, sales can be generated by displaying merchandise.

As we have seen, most of the earlier work in inventory theory has been in the manufacturing industry. One of the main reasons for this is the close interaction between production engineering and operations research. The technical background of the people in the production area has made it easier for them to accept mathematical models. It is also easier to get data for such applications and to demonstrate the worth of the models. Mathematicians and economists made their entry into inventory theory more recently and have concentrated their efforts on the mathematical and economic interpretations of the models.

Many of the inventory control systems that have been developed are based on models which use a cost minimization approach. The inputs to the model are the different cost coefficients and the supply schedule (quantity discounts, lead time, etc.). The outputs of the model are reorder quantity and reorder time.

Classification

One dimension that can be used to classify inventory models is the demand pattern for the items. A "staple" item, according to Webster, is "any chief item of trade, regularly stocked and in constant demand." Constant demand here implies that the item is in demand throughout the year and the coefficient of variation (standard deviation/mean) of demand is small. Fashion items, on the other hand, are in demand only during a certain time span, known as the "season," during the year. After the end of the season the demand for the item (if any), will be many orders of magnitude below the demand during the season. This classification has an effect on the time horizon considered in model building. Inventory models for staple items are usually for a very long time horizon, perhaps on the order of a few months, or even several years. The time span in inventory models for fashion items is usually much shorter, usually a few weeks. Consequently, there should be very few or no reorders for fashion items. Furthermore, the reorder decision must be made very early in the season when it is relatively difficult to predict the nature of demand for the item.

The physical life time of an item, as measured by its propensity to deteriorate or degrade over time, is another important dimension that affects inventory modeling. Some items can be stored for a long period of time without undergoing physical change. These are called "nonperishable" items. On the other hand, "perishable" items have a much shorter life span because they do physically deteriorate over a period of time, making them unfit for consumption. Items that are past their life time may have to be disposed of at ridiculously low prices or at a loss.

Table 2.1 gives examples of items classified according to their demand and physical life time characteristics.

Some other dimensions that can be used to classify inventory models are:

(1)   Lead time for delivery of the items after placement of the order
(2)   Handling of shortages — whether excess demand (demand that cannot be met immediately from current inventory) is backlogged or lost, or partly backlogged and partly lost
(3)   Each of these characteristics — demand, life time, and lead time — can be treated as a deterministic or as a stochastic variable. It is much

simpler to deal with deterministic models since they are limiting cases of stochastic models.

The subsections that follow will take a brief look at each of the categories defined above.

(S,NP) Items

Inventory theory has been well developed for staple, nonperishable (*S,NP*) items. Most of the intermediate products in manufacturing industries and quite a few consumer items fall into this category. Well-known inventory models in this area are the *production lot size* models and the (*s,S*) *periodic review* models. A major portion of the book by Hadley and Whitin [15] deals with models for (*S,NP*) items. Veinott [40] has surveyed the status of mathematical inventory theory. Bellman et al. [2] give a dynamic programming formulation of the general decision-making problem for an item facing an uncertain demand. They also analyze special cases of this general problem. In all these approaches, the basic underlying assumption is that the inherent value of the item in inventory does not change over time. This assumption is not appropriate for fashion items, which require a basic difference in model formulation.

An IBM applications package, IMPACT [18] — "Inventory Management Program and Control Techniques" — is based on models developed for (*S,NP*) items. IMPACT is therefore inadequate for nonstaple items.

(F,NP) Items

A large number and variety of items fall into the fashion, nonperishable (*F,NP*) category. Fashion garments and Christmas cards are two examples. There is a demand for such items only during a short season in the year, and the items do

Table 2.1. A Classification Scheme

Physical Life Time	Demand Structure	
	Staple Item (*S*)	Fashion Item (*F*)
Nonperishable (*NP*)	(*S,NP*) Steel, Sugar	(*F,NP*) Fashion Garments Christmas Cards
Perishable (*P*)	(*S,P*) Human Blood Vegetables	(*F,P*) Christmas Trees Easter Lilies

not physically perish. Inventory models for such items are usually referred to as *models of obsolescence*. Relevant inventory models for such items are presented later in this chapter.

(S,P) Items

Human blood is an example of a staple perishable (S,P) item. There is a year-round demand for blood, which makes it a staple item. It is perishable, since bacterial growth makes it unfit for transfusion twenty-one days after it is drawn. Nahmais [26], who has surveyed perishable inventory theory, states (p. 2) that "models of obsolescence are fundamentally different from those for perishable and decaying inventories in that once items become obsolete, they are not reordered." The main problem in blood-bank perishable inventory theory is keeping track of the physical age distribution of the items in inventory. Another question of interest in perishable inventory theory is the optimal issuing policy to deplete the items from inventory. These issues are not as important for fashion, nonperishable items.

(F,P) Items

Christmas trees, Easter lilies and Easter eggs are a few examples of fashion, perishable (F,P) items. The distinction between obsolescence of an item and its physical perishability is not too clear in the literature. This distinction is important because of the need to keep track of the age distribution of items in inventory as well as the time to obsolescence in models for (F,P) items. It makes the analysis quite complicated and there are no models in the literature that deal specifically with this problem. It is an area that is still open to research.

Inventory Models for (F,NP) Items

The sections that follow examine several models that have been developed for (F,NP) items. Each model will be examined to determine if it is appropriate for fashion garments.

The Newsboy Problem

One of the earliest models developed in the (F,NP) category was for the "newsboy problem." In this problem, an item has a stochastic demand schedule and a different value or worth before and after it becomes obsolete. The model gives the optimum inventory for maximizing expected profits.

Certain characteristics of the newsboy model make it unsuitable for application to other (F,NP) items such as fashion garments. There is no reorder decision in the newsboy model, and all that matters is the initial order quantity.

The selling price and salvage value are given, and there is no time and no opportunity to reduce prices and have a clearance sale. An underlying assumption in this model is that the scenario will be repeated a large number of times — just as a newsboy sells newspapers over a number of days. With a stationary demand distribution (when the demand distribution does not change from one day to the next), the expected profit will be maximized by carrying the optimum stock obtained from the model. However, for fashion garments the demand distribution changes appreciably over time.

The newsboy model assumes the capability of the seller to sustain and survive a string of losses which would be overtaken by profits in the long run. This assumption is suspect when large amounts of money are involved, as the risk aversion of the firm may then become an important factor. The firm may prefer a satisficing objective over a maximizing one.

The Whitin Model

Whitin [37] assumes that the probability distributions of the mean demand for an item at different prices are known. His solution is to apply the standard Economic Order Quantity inventory model (EOQ) at a given selling price, and to find the reorder quantity that maximizes profits. This process is repeated for different prices. The price which offers the maximum profit potential is the optimal price. In certain cases, the two-step optimization can be handled by a simple mathematical function. Using elementary calculus, the optimal price and optimal quantity can be found.

The Whitin model is theoretically sound, but difficult to implement. Even if retailers maintain historical information, the only data that they may have for a style item is that for the performance of similar items in the previous season(s). They would thus have sales data at only a few specific price levels that were fixed for the item, making it unlikely that the basic input to the model — probability distributions of mean demand at different prices — could be easily obtained. Getting the price response function (expected demand as a function of price) is a problem in itself. Though the model is very simplistic (it ignores a number of realistic problems such as lead time), it is a step in the right direction.

The Hertz and Schaffir Model

Hertz and Schaffir [17] have developed a forecasting model for seasonal style-good inventories. The first part of the model is the classical newsboy model that gives the optimum number of items to carry. In the second part of the model, the authors develop a sales forecasting procedure for a particular line of items for the season. They employ a sales growth curve that has a cumulative normal distribution. This gives the fraction of total sales that is expected to take place at the end of each period. This fraction is called the "forecasting ratio," g_i. The total sales for the season, forecasted in period i, S_i, can be found by dividing the sales to date, s_i, by the forecasting ratio, i.e., $S_i = s_i/g_i$. Because the sales to date can vary about the normal growth curve due to totally random factors, there is a distribution of actual cumulative sales around the expected cumulative sales. Furthermore, there is uncertainty about the true value of the forecasting ratio, g_i, because a priori the true value of the total sales for the season is not known. The problem is complicated by the fact that the length of the season is not known with certainty. Though the end of the season is usually fixed, there is some uncertainty about the beginning of the season. This uncertainty will be reflected in the value of the total sales of the season, S_i, which will have its own distribution.

Hertz and Schaffir have empirically found the distribution of g_i for different periods in the season and have discovered that its coefficient of variation falls sharply during the central third of the season. This should result in increasingly better estimates for total sales for the season as the end of the season nears.

From this framework, a method for estimating total season sales is given. A priori estimates of the total season sales are required. Exact values for both the cumulative sales to date and the time remaining until the end of the season can be easily obtained. For each estimate of total season sales, the fraction of total sales achieved as a function of the time to the end of the season is plotted. The curve that most closely follows the hypothesized normal growth pattern gives the best estimate of total season sales and the length of the season.

This model has an inherent shortcoming, in that there is no linkage between its parts. Suppose the manufacturer or the buyer (for a retail store) obtains the optimum quantity from the first part and the weekly forecast of total season sales from the second part. How would he or she reconcile these two figures? Furthermore, the authors do not give the buyer any guidelines for how many orders to place in the season, the size of the orders, and the timing of the orders (assuming the buyer has a choice). Also, the model is structured for a product line that follows the normal growth curve. This may not be a good assumption for fashion garments. No allowance is made for any interaction between inventory and sales. The model was developed to help a textile manufacturer control finished stocks of style goods. Because the demand phenomena at the retail level are very different from those at the manufacturing level, the model is not appropriate at the retail level.

The Cyert Study

Cyert et al. [10] have conducted an in-depth study of the retail ordering and pricing processes in a specific department of a retail store. Their study provides insight into the actual functioning and decision-making process in the department. It is a descriptive (positive) model and does not give any normative solution to the problem. They do not claim to do, or attempt to do, any sort of optimization. It is, however, a very important and interesting piece of work.

The authors found that ordering decisions have two major objectives: they limit markdowns to an acceptable level; and they maintain inventory at a reasonable level. Initial orders and reorders depend on different sets of variables. Initial orders reduce the uncertainty for the department and its suppliers by providing a contractual environment. The department can benefit from a wider selection of merchandise before the beginning of the season. Suppliers usually offer incentives for advance orders by providing favorable credit terms and extra services. Reorders are a function of the actual performance of the item through the season, and supplier constraints such as lead time. Reorders contribute almost all of the variance in the total orders for the season.

The department has a six-month planning horizon and sales forecasting is done for each month. Orders are based upon the sales estimates for each season which are obtained by applying simple "rules of thumb" to the actual dollar sales figures in the corresponding period of the previous year. The department recognizes four main seasons — Easter, summer, fall, and holiday. The initial order quantity is some fraction of the dollar sales estimate for each season. For the particular department under study, these fractions are 0.5, 0.6, 0.75 and 0.65 respectively, for each season. The value of the fraction is indirectly related to the susceptibility of seasonal sales to exogenous variables such as the weather or the "specialty" characteristics of the merchandise.

The reorder quantity for each product class is found by the following rule:

$$R_{(T-t)} = \frac{s_t \, s_{(T-t)}}{S^t} + M - I_t$$

where t = time from beginning of season to date; s_t = last year's sales in time t; T = length of season; $s_{(T-t)}$ = last year's sales in time $(T-t)$; S_t = this year's sales to date, i.e., up to time t; $R_{(T-t)}$ = reorder estimate; M = minimum stock requirement; and I_T = available stock at t, including merchandise on order. If $R_{(T-t)}$ is negative, no reorders are placed. In addition, action is taken to reduce the excess stock by renegotiating contracts with suppliers, canceling previous orders, transferring merchandise to other parts of the firm when possible, or marking down merchandise to stimulate sales.

The three different pricing situations are: (1) normal pricing, (2) sale pricing, and (3) markdown pricing. Pricing procedures are based mainly upon informal guidelines. Normal pricing for standard items is found by charging a 40% markup on cost and adjusting the figure to the nearest $0.95 ending. Higher markups are allowed for exclusive and imported items. Sale pricing is based upon standard schedules: a standard reduction on the regular price or a lower markup on cost. Markdowns are taken at certain times to clear normal remnants, overstocked merchandise, and unacceptable (defective) merchandise. At times, markdowns are taken to accommodate fresh inventory or to keep within the financial limits set for the department as measured by the "open-to-buy" dollar figure. The first markdown is established by reducing the retail price by 1/3 and carrying the result to the nearest $0.85 ending. Higher priced items are marked down 40%.

The model was tested on real data and found to accurately predict the actual ordering and pricing decisions. It is interesting to note that of the pricing decision models, markdown pricing had the poorest record — only 88% accurate predictions, compared to 95.4% for markup and about 98% for sale pricing. This could indicate that markdown pricing is a much more complicated process than the other two. The authors observe that second and succeeding markdown prices, Y, are related to the initial markdown price, X, by the top half of the parabolic curve $Y^2 = 5 (X - 2)$. This very interesting relationship shows that the higher the initial markdown, the greater the reduction in succeeding markdown prices.

The main advantage of this model is the potential saving in manpower as a result of computerization of these decision processes. Buyers and other personnel can then devote their energies to areas that require human judgment and management.

The Brown Model

Brown et al. [5] have developed a model to optimize inventory costs in the presence of stochastic obsolescence of inventory. It is assumed that there are many possible states of nature, each of which results in a different demand. One of these states can be the "obsolescence state" for which the demand is zero. The a priori probabilities of being in each state are known. Furthermore, the probabilities of switching from one state to another are given by a Markovian transition probability matrix. The probability of being in a state in any period is obtained from the observables in the previous period and the transition matrix by applying Bayesian procedures. The authors use the dynamic programming algorithm for this problem to determine the optimal stocking policy.

There are some difficulties in using this approach for the fashion merchandising problem. The transition probability matrix can be expected to change very rapidly from one period to the next because of the peculiar nature of the sales growth curve. This complicates the analysis because an "n" period problem may have up to (n-1) transition matrices. In practice, it would be very difficult to get values for these matrices.

The Barankin and Denny Model

Barankin and Denny[1] compare the optimal inventory policies for an item with and without the presence of obsolescence probabilities. In the model with obsolescence, the item could become obsolete in any period with some known probability. It can then be sold at some salvage price. Using a dynamic programming formulation, the optimal ordering policy is found to be of the (s,S) type for both these models. The authors compared the two models for an exponential demand distribution and some specific values for the cost parameters. They found that for each period, the (s,S) levels for the obsolescence model were lower than those for the ordinary model. This result should be intuitively obvious considering the uncertainty involved in the obsolescence case.

Pierskalla [31] reports some computational experience with the Barankin model and some of the mathematical ramifications. His examples show that as the number of periods in the model is increased, the critical number (i.e., the starting stock in each period after reordering) for the obsolescence cases asymptotically approach the critical numbers when there is no obsolescence. When the number of periods is small (one to five periods), there is a wide disparity in the results of the two models.

A similar situation prevails in the retailing of fashion merchandise. The time span is comparatively short, which implies that the number of reorder points is limited. The threat of obsolescence is quite high. However, the nature of the probability distribution for obsolescence is not too apparent, and it may not have an increasing failure rate (IFR). There is a high uncertainty at the beginning of the season as to whether the item will be a success or a failure. The probability of obsolescence does increase towards the end of the season. It is also possible to change obsolescence probabilities by changing control variables such as price. The problem is further complicated because demand is a function of the period (there is a nonlinear sales growth), and therefore is not independent and identically distributed in every period.

The Murray Model

Murray et al. [25] present a dynamic programming formulation of the style goods inventory problem. They develop their model from the micro level of a potential customer to the macro level of the firm. The number of potential customers, N, and the probability, p, of a potential customer selecting the item under consideration over other competing items, is assumed to be known at some point in time. The number of potential customers and the number of customers who actually buy this item are observed over succeeding time periods. The probability density function, p, is modeled as a two parameter beta function. Based upon the information gained in the current period and using Bayesian theory, its current value is revised. The authors then formulate a dynamic programming model where the stages are the reorder points and the states are the entering stock levels from the previous period. They present a computational shortcut for large problems by reducing the state space.

The practical applicability of this model is questionable. In a retail situation, it is very difficult to obtain data on the number of potential customers. The sales data reflect the actual purchases of the item, i.e., the product of N and p, and it is difficult to separate the two. Furthermore, the assumption of a constant p for all potential customers is a very strong one. The probability p conceivably takes into account the demand function. The authors ignore the problem of predicting N for each time period.

The Wolfe Model

Wolfe's model [39] for style merchandise inventory planning is based on his hypothesis that sales in the season are proportional to the quantity of merchandise displayed, for certain types of style merchandise. Using this hypothesis, he derives the inventory policy and the optimal markdown timing. The model lacks empirical validity because the basic hypothesis was never tested.

In this model, the time between placement of the order and its receipt, i.e., the lead time, is implicitly assumed to be zero. If this assumption were relaxed and the lead time were not zero, the inventory, I_r, just before the receipt of the reorder would be assumed to be known with certainty. So there is a problem of forecasting the value of I_r. The inventory, I_r, will not be a constant and will have a distribution. This uncertainty is completely ignored in this model.

The model is based on the assumption that the buyer knows the values of the sales constants, k_i. In actual practice, there is a high degree of uncertainty about the values of k_i (sales to inventory ratio in period i) for fashion garments, especially at the beginning of the season. As the season progresses, better estimates of k_i based on the sales data can be obtained.

A Broadcast Spot Pricing Model

Lodish [23] formulates a dynamic programming model for the pricing of TV and radio advertisement spots over time. The formulation of this problem is quite straightforward.

The inherent nature of the problem considerably simplifies its solution. The broadcast timing of a particular spot is known in advance and thus its "life time" is known with certainty. If the spot is not sold, its salvage value is zero. Furthermore, there are industry norms on the range of acceptable prices that can be charged for time spots at specific times in the day and during specific programs. These conditions definitely do not hold true for fashion garments.

A broadcast spot is either sold or not sold, whereas the depletion of a fashion garment inventory is a continuous process that necessitates considerable bookkeeping. There is a great deal of uncertainty about the life of a fashion garment, although an upper limit can be placed (based on the definition of a season). After the item is introduced in the stores, current sales data can be used to update the estimates of its life. Institutional pricing (as in broadcast spot pricing) is a different process than pricing for individual customers, where psychological considerations can be important.

These factors make the dynamic programming solution for a fashion garment a much more complex task. The number of items handled by a buyer is also quite large (two hundred to four hundred at any point of time); and the application of a dynamic programming algorithm would be very inefficient.

Some Pricing Considerations

Though pricing theory has long been dominated by economists, psychologists have recently ventured into this area. Retailers have been aware of the importance of taking psychological considerations into account in their pricing decisions. Nevertheless, the economists' ideas on price have dominated the field in marketing practice as a result of their "neat" mathematical models. The economists picture the consumer as a rational economic man who precisely gauges the effects of his budget allocation decisions on his overall "utility" and makes rational decisions. This may not be true in actual practice. To the consumer, price may connote things other than the economic worth of the product. Price may convey some information about the quality of the product: a higher priced product may be perceived to be of better quality than a lower priced one. Reducing the price below a certain level may have a negative effect on sales. This conflicts with economic theory.

Cooper [9], on the basis of limited experimentation, comes up with some interesting results on the psychological significance of price. He hypothesizes that the relationship between perceived quality and price is logarithmic: *Quality* $= k$ log (*price*). This equation implies that, above a certain price threshold, the customer perceives smaller and smaller quality improvements when prices are increased by the same dollar amount. Below this price threshold, perceived quality is much more sensitive to small changes in price.

Cooper's second result concerns the "bargain" price for an item. He concludes (p. 116) that "price reductions tend to be perceived absolutely rather than relatively. This means that the percentage reduction decreases for the item to be considered a bargain as the usual price increases...." This should have important implications in formulating a markdown policy.

Practical Implications and Research Perspective

It is inappropriate to apply inventory models that were developed for manufacturing applications to the fashion retailing area. For fashion garments the market is not perfectly competitive and the retailer may not have a perfectly elastic demand schedule. The practice of fixing the selling price according to existing markup models and then applying inventory theory to find the reorder policy may not be optimal. It might be necessary to link the demand and supply aspects of the problem.

The other aspect of inventory planning for fashion garments is sales forecasting. Usually, there is a great deal of uncertainty as to how an item will fare in the market since there are no previous sales data for a new style item. Hence the size of the initial order is an especially difficult and critical issue to be resolved. However, as the season progresses, the current sales data may be used to get a better estimate of the probable sales for the item. Bayesian statistical theory is the tool that is commonly used for this purpose. It has been incorporated in some of the models in the literature — notably in the Hertz and Schaffir model [17] and the Hartung model [16]. Knowledge about the nature of the stochastic demand process for (F, NP) items, however, is still lacking.

3

Institutional Structure in Fashion Merchandising

In order to come to grips with the multidimensional challenges in predicting fashion demand, it is important to understand the institutional structure for the merchandising of (F, NP) items at the retail level. For this purpose, a large West Coast promotion-oriented chain department store, dealing mainly in soft goods, was selected. This chapter describes the company and its buying process. The information here is based upon discussions and interviews with buyers from five different departments of this company.

Organizational Setup

This particular department store caters mainly to middle and upper middle income families. Its philosophy with regard to fashion merchandising is summed up in a statement made by one of the managers: "We would like to be one breath away from the leader in fashions." The implication is that the store does not like to take a high degree of risk by "creating" fashions. Rather, it prefers to wait and see the trend in fashions and then enter the market as soon as possible thereafter with the "hot selling" items.

At the onset of this study, the chain was comprised of approximately seventy stores spread throughout California and a few neighboring states. The head office has a Central Buying Department and a Warehouse/Distribution Center. Each store is divided into a number of departments such as Men's, Women's, Women's Sportswear, Children's, Junior's, etc. Each department has a buyer who selects, buys, and manages (pricing, promotions, markdowns, quantity decisions, etc.) all items in that department for all seventy stores. There are approximately seventy-five buyers for the company. A buyer has a staff of one or two assistant buyers and one or two distributors. There is a wide disparity in the nature of business in each of these departments, since each caters to a different customer base having different needs. However, because they are part of the same organization, the departments also have some common denominators in their operational setup.

The Buying Function

This section examines the buying function in this particular organization in more detail.

Item Classification

The buyer categorizes items by class and subclass. Classification schemes and purposes may differ by department, and by buyer. The buyer might want a group of items to be housed or displayed together in the stores. Putting these in the same class simplifies this task. A class can also delineate a set of similar items in the same "price-line." For example, all printed T-shirts retailing at $9.95 could be put in a class. Each class is divided into subclasses which are based on the look of the garment. Within each subclass there are individual items which are the basic SKUs (stock keeping units). There are no strict guidelines for assigning SKU numbers to incoming merchandise. A buyer has full control of this task. There could be 150 to 400 SKUs in a department at any point in time.

An SKU number may be an item from a particular vendor and may include a number of color/size combinations. For certain items (such as dress shirts) it may be useful to keep track of sales by color of the item. In such cases SKU numbers are assigned by color. This simplifies the task of clearing slow-moving colors by promoting items in only these colors.

Certain reordered items may be assigned new SKU numbers, so as to differentiate between the old and new stock. The older merchandise is shop-worn and consists of a broken assortment. Assigning a new SKU number becomes useful when the item has a long life-span and it is necessary to clear the old inventory of the item by marking it down. Reordered items may have minor differences from the initial order and may also be different in terms of the color/size assortment. This also prompts some buyers to assign new SKU numbers to reorders.

For example, in the Women's Dresses department, the classes could be based on the silhouette or look of the garment (long dresses, petite sizes, and pant-suits). Each of these is a specialized business in itself. Within the petite size range there are subclasses: social dress, pant-suits, and casual day wear. The social dress subclass will have a number of items from different vendors which will form the basic SKUs.

The Planning Process

The buying process starts with a season plan. This plan is very important because receipts of merchandise are based on it. For domestic purchases, the season plan is generally made about six months in advance. For imported goods the planning horizon is longer (nine months to a year), since the lead time for receipt of merchandise is longer.

Most buyers in this company believe that the concept of a season has recently become less important. This is a consequence of a general change in the behavior of customers, who today buy garments only when they need them. They do not consciously plan to acquire a wardrobe for the next "season." Buyers, therefore, try to "create" seasons. As one buyer put it, "the length of the season is as long as you want to make it!" The buyers try to tempt customers by constantly trying to give a new look to the inventory on display.

The company has set up six-month periods — February to July, and August to January — as its planning units. A department can have two to four seasons in the year, i.e., spring, summer, fall, and holiday, during which there is a change in the look of the merchandise sold in the department. The changeover to a new season is a gradual process. For example, in some departments, the spring merchandise is brought in around December, when there is still a good deal of fall merchandise on the shop floor.

The company relies mostly on its own historical data and internal information when formulating its plans. It gives the least weight to outside sources of information. The buyers receive the company plan, which is a cumulative of the planned percentage increase or decrease for each department over the previous year's actual sales, and the planned expansion in business by the opening of new stores. They also get a suggested department plan along with information on the previous year's actual sales by class, and by subclass for their departments.

The buyers first add or delete classes based upon their expectations of future trends in their particular line of merchandise. An experienced buyer also looks for patterns in demand for items. The buyers claim that there is a five- to seven-year cycle in which fashions tend to repeat themselves. Buyers who have been in the same department for a long enough time could make profitable use of their knowledge of past history.

The total planned dollar sales are next modified by the buyer to fit company and department expectations as well as the calendar for the current year. These adjustments are made to take into account any special events and the shift in holidays (such as Easter and Father's Day) to a different week or month. Such changes drastically affect the weekly and/or monthly sales and are crucial for planning the receipt of merchandise at the correct times.

Generally speaking, buyers prefer to have a conservative plan. For example, a buyer may expect a 20% increase in sales for the department over last year's sales. However, the buying plan will be based on only an 18% increase in sales. The total planned dollars are then allocated to different classes. Certain classes are bound to perform better than expected and others will perform as expected or below. The 2% cushion provides the buyer with some flexibility and enables him or her to devote more dollars to the better performing categories.

The Buying Process

The actual buying process is perhaps the most creative aspect of a buyer's job, and the one which should take the most time and energy. (This challenge will not be addressed in the present study.) After an item is selected, the buyer must decide the quantity and the time schedule for receipt of the merchandise. The retail price of each item must also be determined.

Lead times for delivery of merchandise depend on a number of factors, such as the geographic location of the vendors, the peculiar character of the department, the overall demand for the item among competing retailers, and the vendor's perception of the importance of the buyer among his (the vendor's) customers. Table 3.1 gives an indication of the typical lead times for delivery of merchandise based on the location of the supplier.

After the merchandise is received, the distributor (with the help of the buyer) allocates the item to the company's different stores. The distribution center then tickets, packs, and transports the items to the stores. The lead time for items to be placed on the shop floor after leaving the distribution center varies from one to fourteen days. This is a function of the distance of the store from the distribution center and the availability of floor space in the store.

Markups

The markup for each item is set by the buyer. There are no set guidelines on the quantum of markups. However, there are certain general considerations:

(1)   The company's philosophy is to give its customers "the best quality at the best price"

(2)   The price has to be competitive. The vendors are a good source of information in this regard. The buyers also do some comparative shopping to gauge the marketplace

(3)   The buyers feel that too many different prices in the department create managerial and operational problems. They prefer to have a few "price-lines." The markup on any particular item is such that the price falls into one of these price-lines. Such price-lines have traditionally been popular in the fashion retailing industry and consist of prices ending in 95 or 99 cents; for example $39.95, $14.99, and $7.99.

Table 3.1   Lead Time for Orders

Vendors Based In	Lead Time (Weeks)
Outside US	24 - 36
New York	4 - 8
Los Angeles	2 - 4
San Francisco	1 - 2

The markups for most items are between 100% and 140% of cost. The planned gross margin for a class also affects the current markup on an item. The actual gross margin on a class may be falling behind the planned margin because of a large number of markdowns on some items in that class. In this case, some buyers try to take a higher markup on a new items in that class to compensate for the lower margin realized to date.

Monitoring Performance

Once the item is placed on the shop floor the buyer must monitor its performance so as to take timely action to reprice, promote, reorder, or cancel future deliveries and take markdowns. Some of these aspects are covered in more detail in later sections.

To monitor performance, the buyer must obtain sales data for the item. The company has a very good data collection network. Each store has a number of point-of-sale terminals which are connected by telephone lines to a central computer in the head office. All sales are registered on the point-of-sale terminals which transmit the data to the central computer that updates the data base. The data base has sales and inventory data on each item for the current week, and for the past three weeks, arranged by store. These figures are put together in a "Style Status Detail Report" and given to the buyers and distributors every week. Summary reports by class and price-line are also generated. These reports theoretically allow the buyer to identify slow-moving merchandise and also to determine which stores are below and above the average sales rate.

In some departments (for example, children's wear), the performance by vendor is supposed to convey more information to the buyer than a performance report by individual style. Historically, some vendors have a better performance record than others. In such a situation, the buyers can obtain reports that group items by vendors.

A fashion item that is continually showing around a twenty week supply (or worse) is considered to be a "slow" item. A "good" item is one that shows a six to eight week supply (or better). The buyers think that it takes around eight weeks to really "test" an item. Thus, judging items as fast or slow sellers only on the basis of their turnover rate presents problems. Most buyers said that they use their instincts based on their previous experience to help them evaluate items.

Reorders

For fashion garments, the percentage of reorders to initial orders is very small. In some departments, there are almost no reorders. The reorder decision for fashion merchandise is more complex than that for staple items.

A fashion item that is having a six- to eight-week inventory turnover is considered to be a good candidate for a reorder. However, there are factors other than turnover that must be considered. These include the length of time the item has been on the shop floor, the current position of the item in its fashion life cycle (rise or decline) and in the season (beginning or end). A wrong decision to reorder is very expensive to the buyer. As one of the buyers put it: "It is the last reorder that kills you."

Strategies to Deal with Slow-Moving Items

Theoretically, a buyer has alternative strategies available should it become necessary to dispose of slow-moving merchandise.

Redistribution of Merchandise

In a multistore organization such as the one under investigation, each store exists in a different environment and the sales performance of an item can vary widely from store to store. Hence a buyer can transfer inventory from a store where the item is performing poorly to a store where it has a higher sales rate. On the average, it takes two weeks to pack, transport, unpack, and display the merchandise in the other store. Consequently, the item will be losing two weeks of display, and the cost of transfer will be incurred. Thus, a store-to-store transfer may prove uneconomical unless there is a large difference in the sales rate for the item between the stores, and substantial quantities of the item are involved.

Another negative aspect of merchandise transfer is that the goods shipped are usually "unbalanced" in terms of color-size combinations, and may be shop-worn. This results in behavioral problems, and the store that receives the transferred items may resist the transfer of these items and indirectly sabotage their performance.

The buyers try to keep transfers to a minimum. Thus the initial distribution of merchandise among stores becomes very important. The distributor in the buyer's department plays a key role in this matter.

Storing Goods for the Next Season

For a staple item having a seasonal sales pattern, storage might be a very good strategy. However, storing a fashion item is a very high risk proposition because the odds of the same fashion becoming a good seller in the next year are usually small. (As stated earlier, the buyers believe that there is a five- to seven-year fashion cycle.) The capital cost for storing such inventories is very high due to the length of time involved. Consequently, this alternative is rarely practiced.

Returning Merchandise to Vendor

Recourse to this strategy depends on the contract between the buyer and the vendor. Generally, defective merchandise and merchandise not up to specifications can be returned to the vendor. The retailer is expected to bear the risk of poor performance of items.

Pricing

A multistore organization can have either a uniform pricing policy for all of its stores, a policy for groups of stores, or each store can have its own pricing policy. The organization can also have a combination of uniform pricing and store-specific pricing depending on the length of time an item has been in the store and the inventory on hand. A uniform pricing policy simplifies the administrative task of the buyer. These strategies are discussed in more detail in the next section.

Retail Adjustments and Markdowns

As mentioned earlier, this particular company is a promotion oriented department store. Therefore, changing prices is a very important tool used by the buyer to control inventory levels. The price change could be either temporary (for promotional purposes) or permanent (a markdown). All prices until the first markdown are set by the buyer. The buyers usually look at the performance of an item at the company level (as opposed to the data at the store level) before deciding on promotional and markdown strategies for an item. This is understandable considering the large number of items handled by a buyer.

Retail Adjustment

A promotional price reduction in this company, known as a "retail adjustment", involves the following:

(1) The price reduction is usually advertised in a weekly tabloid which is mailed to customers

(2) Generally, similar items in the same price line are promoted at the same time. This is supposed to reduce any negative association in quality that a lower priced item may have

(3) These promotions are generally planned up to four weeks in advance to allow enough time to prepare the advertisements, print the tabloid, and mail it to the customers in time. This requires the buyer to do some forecasting (which may be pure guesswork) to predict the future performance of an item and similar items in the same price line

Since promotional items are usually advertised, it is difficult to separate the effect of price promotion on sales from the effect of the advertisement. The buyers also claim that there is a positive impact on sales in a class by promoting a subclass within this class. This effect is also difficult to measure.

Markdowns

Markdowns are very important to the buyer since the profitability of the department depends on the number and length of markdowns taken. Markdowns are usually perceived to be a negative policy. Used judiciously, however, they can minimize losses.

Once an item is marked down, the stores take it off the floor and it gets no exposure. The buyers lose control of the item. At this point, the most important incentive to the customer to buy the item is its price.

The buyer uses markdowns for a variety of reasons. They are a way to speed the sale of slow-moving, damaged, or out-of-season merchandise and to make room for new goods coming in. A continual flow of fresh merchandise helps move the "odds and ends" in the department. The department becomes "exciting" and customers come in to see the new merchandise. Markdowns also release capital tied up in obsolete inventory and invest the funds in more salable and profitable merchandise.

Sources of markdowns vary and can be any one, or a combination, of the following factors. These items could be remainders from a promotional or a special purchase; the type of fabric, quality, style or pattern, color, sizes — any one or more of these factors may not be "right" for the season; there may be a huge overstock of the item; the assortment may be broken and shopworn; adjustments may be required to meet competition; the item may have been introduced at the wrong time.

The first markdown is always initiated by the buyer. In most departments it is usually set at a 33% reduction on retail price. The markdown price has to be lower than the lowest price at which the item was promoted earlier in the season, and generally, a 33% reduction ensures this.

Subsequent markdowns are usually taken by the store managers. The buyers can in certain instances take the second markdown, especially when the quantities in stock are substantial. They can also send guidelines to the store managers on the subsequent markdown schedule. The second markdown is usually in the range of 50% of the retail price.

One of the departments follows a different rule to determine the markdown price. Its main objectives are: to have a very simple and fast mechanism to fix the markdown price; and to identify two to three key price-lines of reduced merchandise to customers. To achieve these objectives, the buyer in this department forms groups of merchandise in a certain price range and offers all these at the same markdown price. For example, all garments priced from $26 to $33 are marked down to $19.98. Subsequent markdowns are computed by taking $5 off the current price, usually at four-week intervals.

Company policy requires that when an item is marked down, the old price must be struck off and the new price written on the ticket. This is done manually and is a time-consuming process. The 33% off rule requires more time to implement as compared to the other rule, and the stores supposedly prefer the latter.

Behavioral Aspects of Markdowns

One of the buyers said that there is a tendency to plan markdowns during months in which strong sales are expected. In this way the ($ markdowns/$ sales) ratio is low. This may not be a good policy to follow but is tied in with the buyers' performance evaluation criteria.

There appears to be some dissatisfaction with another criterion used to evaluate buyers: the quantum of dollar markdowns taken. Since the buyer generally has no control over second and subsequent markdowns, the decisions taken by the store managers affect the buyers' evaluation to some extent. The stores are not accountable for the markdowns they take. This is perceived by the buyers to be unfair. One of the buyers said that her most difficult job as a buyer is "controlling the markdowns that the stores take." Estimates given by buyers of the ratio of markdown dollars taken by the buyers to those taken by the stores vary from 60:40 to 70:30.

Only one of the buyers mentioned the valuable information contained in a markdown rack. Looking at these racks gives a very good idea of the likes and dislikes of customers with regard to color and style. It also tells the buyer if he or she is ordering the right assortment by size.

4

Data Collection

The earlier chapters established the need to conduct exploratory research on the structure of demand for fashion items. A major reason for the lack of knowledge of this subject is that capture and storage of data on the large number of sales transactions at the retail level can be a big problem. The primary reason for selecting the company described in chapter 3 is that it has overcome the data storage and capture problem to a certain extent. A good understanding of the data collection procedures in this organization is essential if we are to analyze the data and make inferences on the structure of demand. This chapter will address these issues.

Mechanics of Data Collection

Department Selection

The five buyers interviewed were chosen by management to cooperate with this study because they were perceived as "progressive." These buyers gave the impression that the nature of business was different in each of their departments; and each had his or her own style of managing. In order to broaden the base of this study, it was decided to investigate a few items from each department, a project which involved getting help from the five buyers in several areas.

First, it was necessary to find out the data collection and record keeping procedures in each department so as to be able to interpret the data. This was followed by the selection of a few representative items from each department for tracking over their life time. The final step was the collection of the requisite data for each of the items selected, including: sales by week by store, inventory by week by store, and price by week.

Data Availability

The buyers had different views on the use of historical sales data at the SKU level as a guide to predicting the future demand for similar items. Sales data by store for SKU numbers which are older than four weeks are purged from the computer data base. Therefore, if the buyer wants to maintain his or her own historical data base, the department has to save its weekly computer reports. As a result, data availability varies by department. Two of the buyers thought that historical data were extremely useful and they kept the "Style Status Detail Report" for a previous year or two. This report contains sales and inventory data by SKU number (by store) for the previous four weeks. The three other buyers usually kept only the two most recent reports which contain data for the previous five weeks.

The stores in this company do not have any "back room" inventory. As soon as the store receives a shipment from the distribution center, all the inventory is supposed to be displayed on the shop floor. Therefore, the inventory figures in the reports represent the inventory on display at the beginning of the week.

None of the computer reports carry the actual price at which the items are sold every week. These can be obtained from manual records maintained by the buyers. Because there is no standard procedure for keeping these manual records, there was some difficulty in finding the price data. These records were sometimes not current and were also prone to errors.

Most of the buyers purged or removed an item from the report as soon as the first markdown was taken. They viewed this as a general housekeeping mechanism which kept the reports from becoming voluminous. Also, since the price of the item was set by the store manager after the first markdown, buyers did not want to retain an item in the report over which they had no control.

Item Selection

The buyers were asked to select nine to ten representative fashion items from each of their departments. These items had already been ordered and were supposed to be in the stores in two to three weeks. The distributors were instructed to keep the "Style Status Detail Reports" for these items from the week of their initial introduction into the stores up to the time the first markdown was taken.

In the course of this study, the buyer and/or the distributor in two departments were promoted and posted to other departments. The new personnel were not informed about the study and the need to keep these reports. As a result, data from two out of the five departments were lost. From the remaining three departments, data on twenty-eight items sold in sixty of the chain's seventy stores were obtained. The numbers below give an idea of the volume of data collected.

Number of stores: 60
Number of items: 28

Average number of weeks per item: 20
Number of data points per week: 2

This results in a total of approximately 70,000 data points.

Problems in Data Collection and Analysis

Despite the fact that the company has an on-line real-time system to collect sales and inventory data, a number of problems were encountered.

Time lags. The store inventories are updated as soon as the shipments leave the distribution center though the time required for the items to be actually placed on the shop floor varies by store. An apparent reason for this is the variation in shipment times due to the difference in distances of stores from the central distribution center. A second reason which was not initially apparent is the tendency of some of the stores to hold on to the trucks transporting the items by delaying unloading of the merchandise. The trucks serve as storage areas since the stores have very limited floor space for back-room inventories. The length of time needed for an item to actually reach the shop floor after leaving the distribution center was estimated by the distributors to be anywhere from one to fourteen days. Obviously, such delays falsify inventory figures since the item may not be on the shop floor even though the computer data base shows the contrary.

Reporting errors. In these reports, there were quite a few cases where sales were shown to be greater than the inventory. This could be due either to the miskeying of the item SKU number by the salespeople, or to inventory not being updated in time, especially when there are store-to-store transfers.

Returns. Toward the end of the lifetime of an item, there were a number of instances where sales were shown to be negative. The probable cause for this is that returns from customers were greater than sales for that particular week. It could also be due to miskeying of sales and/or returns.

Markdowns. Data after the first markdown were unavailable as the item was dropped from the data base.

Price data. In certain cases the price data seemed to be in error. This could have been a result of the manual record-keeping system for prices. Evidence of the errors was found on analysis of the raw data.

General Characteristics of the Items

Product Types and Markups

Table 4.1 gives the types of items that were selected for the study and range of their retail prices. Table 4.2 shows the cost, retail prices, and the markup on cost for each of these items. Most of the items have a markup on cost of around 100%. The buyers try to fix the retail price of a new item so that it falls into an existing price-line. This accounts for the slight variance in the markups. There does not seem to be any significant difference in the markups among these three departments.

Markdown Prices, Frequency of Promotions, and Inventory Allocation

Table 4.3 shows the prices of the items after the first markdown and the percentage markdown taken over the retail prices. In most of the cases the data support the findings obtained during interviews with the buyers (see pp. 26-27). Most of the items had around a 33% markdown of the retail price. In fact, out of the seventeen items, ten had markdowns between 30% and 36%, five were between 36% and 39%, and only two were above 40%.

Table 4.4 shows the total weeks until the first markdown and the number and percentage of promotions during this period. There is great variation in promotions of the different items. The numbers below give the minimum, maximum, and average percentage of weeks that an item was promoted in each of the three departments. For example, Department 1 had one item which was promoted 58% of the weeks (the maximum).

Dept.	Minimum	Maximum	Average
1	0	58	31
2	27	50	39
3	13	33	26

Table 4.1   Product Types and Retail Prices

Dept.	Items Selected	Retail Prices
1	Outdoor Women's Shirts: Wide Variety of Styles from Shirts with Laced Cuffs and Collars to "Cowboy" Shirts	$12 to $18
2	Men's Outerwear: Styles from T-Shirts to High Fashion Velour Shirts	$6 to $30
3	Women's Accessories: Fashion Belts, Gloves and Hats	$3 to $16

Table 4.2   Cost, Retail, and Markups

Dept. 1: Women's Sportswear			
Item	**Cost**	**Retail**	**Markup**
1A	5.75	12.00	1.087
1B	4.36	12.00	1.752
1C	5.00	12.00	1.400
1D	5.90	12.00	1.034
1E	6.67	14.00	1.099
1F	7.90	16.00	1.025
1G	7.90	16.00	1.025
1H	7.00	14.00	1.000
1I	7.75	16.00	1.065
1J	8.00	18.00	1.250
1K	8.00	16.00	1.000

Dept. 2: Men's Department			
Item	**Cost**	**Retail**	**Markup**
2B	6.72	14.00	1.083
2C	7.50	15.00	1.000
2D	4.13	10.00	1.421
2F	6.50	13.00	1.000
2G	4.88	13.00	1.664
2H	9.33	20.00	1.144
2I	14.62	30.00	1.052
2J	6.50	14.00	1.154

Dept. 3: Women's Accessories			
Item	**Cost**	**Retail**	**Markup**
3A	4.00	10.00	1.500
3C	1.38	3.00	1.182
3D	2.17	5.00	1.304
3F	3.00	6.00	1.000
3G	2.00	5.00	1.500
3I	3.75	8.00	1.133
3J	6.45	16.00	1.481

The initial inventory and the scheduled delivery of replenishments to the stores are shown in table 4.5. It should be noted here that these replenishments were not "reorders." They were either shipments scheduled when the item was first ordered from the vendors, or inventory in the warehouse that was shipped to the stores at this later date. The buyers said that the percentage of reorders to initial orders was very small. Out of the twenty-six items, eleven had new inventory sent to the stores after the initial receipt.

Table 4.3   Markdown Price and Percentage

Dept. 1: Women's Sportswear

Item	Retail Price	Markdown Price	Markdown Percentage
1A	12.00	7.98	33.5
1B	12.00	7.98	33.5
1C	12.00	7.98	33.5
1D	12.00	7.98	33.5
1E	14.00	8.98	35.9
1F	16.00	9.98	37.6
1G	16.00	9.98	37.6
1H	14.00	8.98	35.9
1I	16.00	9.98	37.6
1J	18.00	9.98	44.6
1K	16.00	9.98	37.6

Dept. 2: Men's Department

Item	Retail	Markdown Price	Markdown Percentage
2D	10.00	6.98	30.2
2F	13.00	7.98	38.6
2G	13.00	6.98	46.3
2H	20.00	12.98	35.1
2I	30.00	19.98	33.4
2J	14.00	8.98	35.9

The allocation of the initial inventory to a store does not seem to have any relationship to the store size. A detailed analysis was conducted for eight out of the twenty-six items. The correlations between these two variables (initial inventory and store size, as measured by floor space area) were very near zero for each of the eight items. The distributors make a standard color-size assortment packet of an item containing a certain number of units. A packet may contain from twelve to eighteen units, depending on the item. Usually one to three of these packets are sent to the stores depending on the buyer's and the distributor's prior expectations of the demand for this item in each store. The median number of units of an item sent to a store is approximately twenty-four.

Table 4.4 Weeks Item Promoted

Dept. 1: Women's Sportswear

Item	Total Weeks	Price Promotion Weeks	Percentage
1A	22	7	31.8
1B	17	8	47.0
1C	12	7	58.3
1D	12	6	50.0
1E	17	6	35.3
1F	22	2	9.1
1G	15	0	0.0
1H	22	9	40.9
1I	21	1	4.8
1K	16	2	12.5
1L	13	7	53.8

Dept. 2: Men's Department

Item	Total Weeks	Price Promotion Weeks	Percentage
2C	25	9	36.0
2D	18	5	27.8
2F	19	8	42.1
2G	19	7	36.8
2H	19	6	31.6
2I	18	9	50.0
2J	11	5	45.5

Dept. 3: Women's Accessories

Item	Total Weeks	Price Promotion Weeks	Percentage
3A	20	5	25.0
3C	13	4	30.8
3D	15	4	26.7
3F	15	2	13.3
3G	15	5	33.3
3I	13	4	30.8
3J	8	2	25.0

Table 4.5. Initial Inventory and Replenishments

Item	Initial Inventory	Replenishments Quantity (Week)		
1A	1200			
1B	6120			
1C	1680			
1D	2088	360 (4)		
1E	2880	3264 (6)		
1F	1440			
1G	1200			
1H	546	2310 (3)	2443 (4)	
1I	966	1204 (4)	2126 (10)	
1J	2400			
1K	912			
2B	3192			
2C	5262	6081 (4)	2448 (9)	351 (15)
2D	4836	2400 (4)	3600 (10)	4800 (14)
2F	3600	2448 (7)		
2G	3060			
2H	3551			
2I	2394			
2J	2760			
3A	1200	1200 (7)		
3C	4080			
3D	2380	2400 (10)		
3F	1800	1800 (10)		
3G	3600	3600 (10)		
3I	2256			
3J	4470			

5

Data Analysis

This chapter addresses the issue raised in chapter 1 regarding the structure of demand for fashion garments. A detailed analysis will be conducted on the sales-to-inventory ratio, and it will be demonstrated that this ratio is an important variable which can be used to manage the demand for fashion items. Several hypotheses will be formulated and tested. The results will increase our knowledge of the structure of the demand for fashion items. Finally, regression analysis will be used to illustrate the relative importance of the determinants of demand in the sales-to-inventory ratio.

Measures of Performance

Many retail organizations use the inventory turnover ratio (the dollar sales volume for the year/average dollar inventory level) as one measure of business performance. There are certain inherent pitfalls in this method. For example, two organizations may have the same inventory turnover ratio in the short run but may be using strategies that could lead to different long-term results. If one uses a low price, high volume strategy, while the other employs a high price, low volume strategy, it is possible that the high price merchandiser may be left with more unsalable or "dead" inventory, and will therefore be at a disadvantage. (This is especially true in the case of fashion merchandise.) The inventory turnover ratio is an average figure that is computed over all items in a department or organization. It usually covers a long time span — typically, a year.

To effectively manage demand, it is necessary to get some feeling for the basic salability of an item on a short term (weekly) basis. Retailers have been using the number of weeks of supply of an item for this purpose. This is found by dividing the unit inventory at the end of the week by the unit sales of the item in the past week. Note that the weeks of supply number does not depend on the monetary value of the item. This is an advantage, especially when there is a wide variation in the cost and retail price of items. The inventory turnover ratio, on the other hand, is influenced to a very large degree by these prices.

An item which has a large number of weeks of supply may or may not be a slow seller. Sales pace depends on a number of factors, such as the current inventory and the position of the item in its life cycle. Therefore, managerial action may or may not be warranted. The weeks of supply concept assumes that the item will exhibit the same unit sales volume in future weeks as it has in the last week. A deeper analysis and understanding of the demand structure is needed in order to manage demand properly.

The Sales to Inventory Ratio: k

One measure of performance which is related to the weeks of supply concept can be defined as

$$k = \frac{\text{Unit sales for the week}}{\text{Unit inventory at the beginning of the week}}$$

Why is k a useful variable? First, note that the initial inventory level and replenishments vary widely over different items (table 4.5). Consequently, unit sales for different items can be expected to exhibit wide variation. This makes the task of comparing the sales performance of items very difficult. One of the biggest advantages of k is its range, which is from 0 to 1.0. Therefore, k could be used to compare the salability of items.

The inventory of an item decreases over time until the next replenishment. This also affects unit sales of the item, complicating the evaluation of the sales performance of an item over time. The variable k is also useful for this purpose. Tracking k across time for an item allows the buyer to monitor the performance of the item over time.

The Variable k *for a Staple Item*

It is interesting to derive the time behavior of k for a staple item and compare this to the plots of k for fashion items. A staple item will have a fairly constant and predictable demand over time, although there may be seasonal and trend elements. There is a certain start-up, or initial, inventory level. The inventory level decreases over time at a constant rate, reflecting the approximately steady sales rate. Therefore, k should increase at an increasing rate over time because the constant sales number will be divided by smaller and smaller inventory numbers. There will be a sudden drop in k when there is a replenishment. This is shown graphically in figure 5.1.

Fig. 5.1. *k* versus Time for a Staple Item

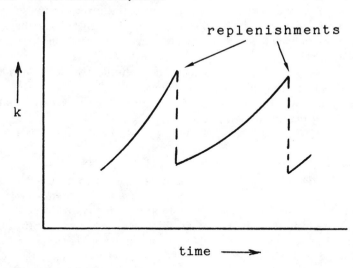

Factors that Affect *k*

The different factors that can affect *k* are the price of the item, time, the depth of stocking the item, prices of competing items in the line, the breadth of the line, and the image of the store and other "macro" factors such as general economic conditions. At the item level, the first three of these factors (price, time, and amount of stock) should affect *k* to a very large degree. These factors will be discussed in more detail in the subsections that follow. From this conceptual basis, hypotheses on the relationship between *k* and these variables will be formulated and statistically tested in later sections. (The last three factors have been included here only for the sake of completeness. The scope of this study and the limitations in the data do not permit exploration of these variables.)

Price of the Item

Price is a very important mechanism that is used to control the sales rate of an item. Next to ordering the right items for a season, determining the optimal prices for the items (regular retail, promotion, and markdown prices) is an important and critical responsibility of the buyer. As is evident in table 4.2, for most items the retail price is based on a standard percentage markup on cost. Similarly, the markdown price is based on a standard percentage markdown on the retail price (table 4.3). The main advantage of this scheme is that it is administratively easy to implement.

The depth and frequency of promotions is a more complex phenomenon. It usually depends on the current sales performance, the buyer's expectations of future sales performance, and the absolute level of inventory for the item. Therefore, promotions will vary from item to item and also from department to department (table 4.4).

Because there is a very close interaction between the price of an item and its attractiveness to customers, price should have a very large influence on the sales rate of an item. For normal goods (in the economist's definition), k should be a decreasing function of price.

Time Effect

When a fashion item is initially introduced, it is expected to have a high sales rate because of its novelty. When a customer buys a fashion item toward the end of its life, it is usable for a shorter duration of time than if it were bought earlier. In other words, the "utility" of a fashion item decreases over time; and thus the inherent demand for a fashion item should decrease as the item becomes older. The demand for a fashion item also depends on special events, such as Christmas and "Back to School" periods, when there is a general surge in the demand for all items.

Based on the above discussion, what can be said about the behavior of k over time? Leaving out the time periods that contain "special events," k should be a decreasing function of time. In other words, a more-than-proportionate decrease in the sales rate of a fashion item is expected, as compared to the decrease in the inventory level.

The decrease in the inherent demand for a fashion item over time has implications on the sales response of the item to promotional price reductions. The increase in k due to promotions should decrease over time, i.e., the first promotion increases k by a larger amount than the second promotion, and so on.

The Depth of Stocking

The distribution of sizes and colors of an item is a very important entity in the marketing of ready-made garments. Carrying an item in different sizes and colors caters to a larger set of customers and reduces the risk to the retailer. Therefore, the retailer must decide on the optimal size-color distribution for the item. This will be referred to as the "depth" of stocking.

As the inventory level is increased, the probability of customers finding the color-size combination of their choice increases (assuming that there is a well-balanced stock). Over the length of the season, some of the color-size combinations will be sold out, and the stock of the item becomes "imbalanced." This (along with the decline due to the inherent decrease in demand) should contribute to the decrease in k for the item over time. When there is a replenishment, a fresh stock of the item is put in the stores. With such an improvement in the assortment, there should be a less-than-proportionate decrease in the sales rate as compared to the decrease in the inventory level. Therefore, k should increase when the item is replenished.

Time Behavior of k

The discussion in the previous section leads to the following two hypotheses:

Hypothesis #1: Excluding special events and holiday seasons such as Christmas, k is a decreasing function of time

Hypothesis #2: Holiday seasons and special events have a positive effect on k

It is informative to take a preliminary look at the plots of k as a function of time. The variable k is based on the sales and inventory data for an item aggregated over all stores. A sample plot is shown in fig. 5.2. (The Appendix contains plots for the items used in this study.) The weekly retail prices of these items are shown on the same plots by dotted lines at the top of the plots. The following observations on the time behavior of k can be made from a visual inspection of these plots:

(1) Time seems to have a substantial impact on k. For most items, k decreases over time, before and after the Christmas season. (The Christmas season has not been formally defined until now; it will be done shortly)

(2) k starts to increase about six to seven weeks before Christmas week. It then drops suddenly just after Christmas. The Christmas season seems to have a positive effect on k.

(3) For some items, k starts at a low level, increases suddenly (maybe for a week or two) and then exhibits a decreasing trend (Item 1D). This could be due to one of two reasons. The first is that some stores may not place the inventory on the shop floor in the same week as the one entered into the computer data base. As a result, without all the inventory being actually on the shop floor, sales would be smaller, resulting in an apparently low k. The other reason is that the sales rate for this item could have required some time (two to three weeks) to pick up momentum. A precise reason for this behavior cannot be assigned, given the deficiencies in the data collection process in this organization.

Fig. 5.2.   Sample Plot of *k* versus Time and Price

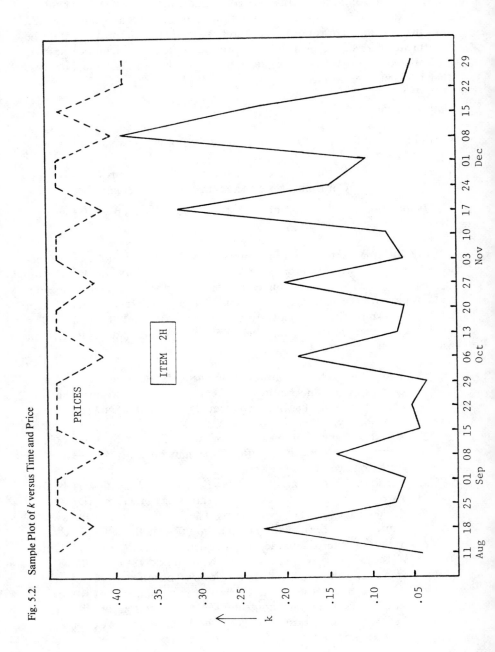

Marking the Beginning of Christmas Season

In testing the first hypothesis, it is necessary to exclude the data points for k that fall in the holiday seasons. Most of the items were introduced in the months of October and November. They were in the stores at least till the end of January. As a result, the data that were collected span the Christmas season. Therefore, the first thing that needs to be done is to define the Christmas season.

At some point in time after the item is introduced and before the week of Christmas, k should be at a minimum. After this, the surge in the inherent demand for most items during the Christmas season should increase the value of k. Define $W_{min\ k}$ to be the week when the item had a minimum k in this period. $W_{min\ k}$ can be approximated as the beginning of the Christmas season. (Since the retail price of the item is changing over time, the minimum k will be based on the weeks during which the item was being sold at its full regular price.)

The histogram of $W_{min\ k}$ is shown in fig. 5.3. Note that there is a variation in $W_{min\ k}$ which is a function of the item (and maybe of the department). For the purposes of testing this hypothesis, a single date that represents the start of the Christmas season is required. The median and mean of $W_{min\ k}$ could be helpful in determining this date. The median of $W_{min\ k}$ is the week beginning November 10, i.e., seven weeks before the week of Christmas. The mean is also around this week. Therefore, November 10 will be assumed to be the beginning of the Christmas season. This date also fits in with what the buyers identified as the beginning of their Christmas season.

Testing Hypothesis #1

Now that the relevant time period has been fixed, the next step is to see how k varies from the time that the item is introduced until the beginning of the Christmas season (November 10). For most items, price is not a constant in this period due to price promotions. There is no mechanism to directly compare k

Fig. 5.3. Histogram of $W_{min\ k}$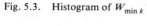

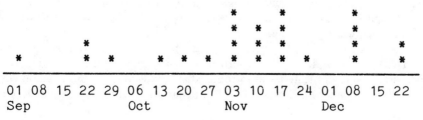

at two different prices. Define k_i as k for the ith instance that the item was sold at a given price. The k_i's can be compared since these are at the same price. Then the first hypothesis translates to:

$$k_i > k_j \text{ for } j > i \qquad (5.1a)$$

or,

$$k_i - k_j > 0 \text{ for } j > i \qquad (5.1b)$$

The null hypothesis is given by $H_0: k$ is a constant over time. For the test procedure, for each i, only the next possible j will be used, and the sign of $(k_i - k_j)$ will be noted. To minimize the possibility of getting spurious associations, the signs of $(k_i - k_j)$ will be taken only when there is a difference of three weeks or less between i and j, i.e., when $j \le i + 3$. At this point, the effect of replenishments on k (discussed earlier, page 40), will be ignored.

Under H_0, if k is assumed to vary randomly (around the constant trend), there should be an equally likely probability that $(k_i - k_j)$ is positive, negative, or zero. The number of $+$ signs in a total of n sign observations will be binomially distributed with probability of a $+$ sign, $p_0 = 0.5$. Therefore, under H_0, an equal number of $+$ and $-$ signs for $(k_i - k_j)$ is to be expected. If the alternate hypothesis is true, the proportion of $+$ signs, p, should be greater than 0.5.

The total number of weeks in the period under investigation, and the number of $+$ and $-$ signs for each item, are shown in table 5.2. When n is large (greater than 10), a normal approximation to the binomial distribution can be used. Under H_0, the number of standard deviations that the observed proportion of $+$ signs, p, is away from the expected, $p_0 = 0.5$, is given by:

$$z_c = \frac{p - p_0}{\sqrt{p_0 (1 - p_0) / n}} \qquad (5.2)$$

The significance probabilities at which H_0 can be rejected on the basis of the observed outcome (i.e., the prob. value) and z_c are shown in table 5.1 for each of the three departments and also for all three departments combined. H_0 can be rejected at a 0.2% level of significance, for Departments 1, 2, and for all three departments combined. However, H_0 cannot be rejected for Department 3, even at a 10% level of significance.

What could be the reason for Department 3 to behave differently? A look at Department 3 shows that fourteen out of the seventeen negative signs occurred just after the item was introduced. The reason(s) for this deviation can only be speculated. Perhaps items in this department require some time to pick

Table 5.1. Test Statistics for Hypothesis #1

Dept.	Total Signs	+ Signs	Proportion + Signs	z_c	Prob. Value
1	44	32	0.727	3.01	0.0013
2	73	49	0.671	2.92	0.0018
3	30	13	0.433	0.73	0.2315
All	147	94	0.639	3.37	0.0004

Table 5.2. Sign of $(k_i - k_j)$ by Item

Item	Total Weeks	Overall + Signs	Overall − Signs	First Three Weeks + Signs	First Three Weeks − Signs	Christmas + Signs	Christmas − Signs
1A	4	2	0	1	0	2	4
1B	6	2	1	0	1	0	5
1C	5	1	1	0	0	4	2
1D	7	4	1	0	1	3	2
1E	8	3	3	1	0	3	2
1F	4	3	0	2	0	3	3
1G	4	3	0	2	0	4	2
1H	8	4	2	0	1	4	1
1I	8	4	3	1	1	2	3
1K	8	6	1	1	1	3	2
2B	4	3	0	1	0	1	6
2C	13	6	3	0	1	2	5
2D	12	4	6	1	1	0	6
2F	14	5	6	0	1	2	3
2G	13	9	2	1	1	1	4
2H	13	5	5	0	1	1	3
2I	13	9	2	0	1	1	4
2J	10	8	0	1	0	*	*
3A	7	3	2	0	2	3	2
3C	5	2	2	1	1	1	4
3D	7	2	4	0	2	1	4
3F	7	3	3	0	2	3	2
3G	7	1	4	0	2	2	4
3I	5	2	2	0	2	2	3

1. The "OVERALL" column gives the number of + and − signs in the "TOTAL WEEKS," which is the time from the first shipment to the beginning of the Christmas season.

2. The "FIRST THREE WEEKS" column gives the number of + and − signs in the first three weeks after the *first* shipment of an item to the stores. This will be used to test the third hypothesis.

3. The "CHRISTMAS" column gives the number of + and − signs in the Christmas season (November 10 to December 22). This will be used to test the third hypothesis.

4. The * for item 2J denotes that the numbers could not be calculated because the item was marked down in this period. Therefore, the prices were not available.

up sales momentum, or it took longer than average for the items in this department to be displayed on the shop floor after being shipped from the warehouse.

Testing Hypothesis #2

The first hypothesis established that k is a decreasing function of time when the holiday season is excluded (this will be referred to as the regular season). If the second hypothesis is true, the holiday season may either reduce the rate of decay, but k may still decrease over time; or halt the decay and k could become steady or increase over time. The null hypothesis will be H_0: Holiday seasons do not have a positive effect on k — there is no difference in the behavior of k over time during the regular and holiday seasons.

The procedure to test this hypothesis is similar to that used to test the first hypothesis. If H_0 is true, there should be no significant difference in the proportion of $+$ (or $-$) signs for $(k_i - k_j)$ during the holiday and regular seasons. If the second hypothesis is true then the proportion of $+$ signs in the Christmas season will be *significantly lower* than the corresponding proportion in the regular season.

Table 5.2 shows the number of $+$ and $-$ signs for $(k_i - k_j)$ during these two periods. Table 5.3 summarizes the test procedure. It shows that the proportion of $+$ signs is indeed lower in the Christmas season. To test for the significance level of the difference between these two proportions, the statistic given in Equation 5.3 is used. This statistic is based on a normal approximation. The proportions in the two samples are p_1 and p_2; and n_1 and n_2 are the number of observations in the two samples.

$$z_c = \frac{p_1 - p_2}{\sqrt{\dfrac{p_1(1 - p_1)}{n_1} + \dfrac{p_2(1 - p_2)}{n_2}}} \tag{5.3}$$

The values of z_c and the prob. values are also given in table 5.3. H_0 can be rejected at a significance level of 1.5% for Department 1 and at 0.01% for Department 2 and for the three departments combined. However, H_0 cannot be rejected for Department 3. Here again, this could be due to the effect of the large number of $-$ signs for items in this department soon after the items were introduced.

Table 5.3.   Test Statistics for Hypothesis #2

Dept.	n_1	Christmas + Signs	Propn.	n_2	Regular + Signs	z_c	Prob. Value
1	54	28	0.481	44	0.727	2.574	0.0053
2	39	8	0.205	73	0.671	5.491	0.0000
3	31	12	0.387	30	0.433	0.365	0.3600
Total	124	48	0.387	147	0.639	4.270	0.0001

Inventory Effect on k

In an earlier section (page 40), the influence of inventory replenishments on k was discussed. This will form the basis of the third hypothesis.

Hypothesis #3: A replenishment has a positive impact on k

Problems in Testing Hypothesis #3

Before testing this hypothesis, it is necessary to note the following problems which were mentioned earlier.

(1)   The exact week that an item is displayed on the shop floor after a replenishment was dispatched from the warehouse cannot be established. This is a problem with the data capturing mechanism in the organization

(2)   A more fundamental problem arises for the holiday season. Since there is an increase in demand during this period, separating the effect of a replenishment from this demand effect is difficult.

To take care of the second problem, the same time period that was used to test the first hypothesis will be utilized to test the third hypothesis (i.e., from introduction of the item to the beginning of the Christmas season).

The first problem poses some difficulties. The ideal situation would be to know the exact date on which the item is put on the shop floor. Since this information could not be easily obtained, the next best thing to do was to consider the behavior of k in the initial few weeks after a shipment was sent, as recorded in the computer data base. Based on estimates of the number of weeks that a shipment took to actually arrive on the shop floor (as given by the distributors in this organization), a three-week period immediately after a shipment seemed to be the appropriate time span to consider. These three-week periods will be referred to as the "replenishment" periods.

Testing Hypothesis #3

Define the "no replenishment" period as the period found by excluding all the "replenishment" periods from the total time span under consideration, i.e., from three weeks after an item is introduced to the beginning of the Christmas season. The signs in this period are shown in table 5.2. (The first three weeks in the item's life cycle are excluded from the analysis to account for the first shipment not being on the shop floor on the day it is shipped. This could result in negative signs for $(k_i - k_{i+1})$. However, this is not the effect of a replenishment.)

The procedure to test this hypothesis is similar to the one used to test the first hypothesis. If this hypothesis is true, the proportion of + signs for $(k_i - k_{i+1})$ in the "replenishment" period, p_r, should be significantly lower than the proportion in the "no replenishment" period, p_{nr}. The total number of + signs in the three-week periods after replenishments is shown in table 5.4. The analysis will be conducted for the three departments combined, since there were not enough replenishments within each department for it to be analyzed in isolation.

Table 5.5 shows the sign count for the "no replenishment" and "replenishment" periods. The proportion of + signs in these periods is given by $p_r = 72/96 = 0.75$, and $p_{nr} = 9/17 = 0.53$. The null hypothesis is H_0; p_r is not significantly different from p_{nr}. The test statistic here is the difference in two proportions given in Equation 5.3. The critical value is given by $z_c = 1.707$. Therefore, H_0 can rejected at a 4.5% level of significance. (Although there is quite a high probability that the third hypothesis is true, a very strong case cannot be made at this point because of the limited data on replenishments. Ideally, in future studies, it would be necessary to get the date that a replenishment was actually placed on the shop floor rather than the date of shipment.)

Effect of Price Promotions on k

When an item is initially introduced, the store will carry a full complement of color-size combinations of that item. Furthermore, because the item is a "novelty" item at that point in time, promotions should have a large positive impact on k. As the item becomes older, it would be "broken" with regard to the color-size assortment and may also have lost some of its fashion status. This may reduce the impact of promotions on k. The fourth hypothesis addresses this issue.

Hypothesis #4:   The effect of a price promotion on k decreases over time in the regular (off-holiday) season

Table 5.4. $(k_i - k_{i+1})$ after a Replenishment

Item	+ Signs	− Signs
1E	1	2
1I	2	1
2C	2	0
	1	0
2D	1	2
	1	2
2F	1	1

Table 5.5. Sign Count for the "No Replenishment" Period

Period	Refer To	+ Signs	− Signs
All Weeks	Table 5.2	94	53
Replenishment	Table 5.4	9	8
First Three Weeks	Table 5.2	13	21
No Replenishment		72	24

The "regular" season which was used to test Hypothesis #1, will also be used to test the fourth hypothesis. Suppose the item was sold at its regular retail price in week t and was promoted in week $t+1$. Let k_t and k_{t+1} be the ks for these two weeks. Then the increase in k is given by:

$$\Delta k_i = k_{t+1} - k_t \tag{5.4}$$

Here, Δk_i represents the change in k when the item was promoted for the ith time (at the same promotion price) in the regular season. Then the hypothesis translates to:

$$\Delta k_1 > \Delta k_2 > \cdots > \Delta k_n \tag{5.5}$$

In other words, the ith promotion will have a larger impact than the $(i+1)$st promotion.

$$\Delta k_i - \Delta k_{i+1} > 0 \quad i = 1, 2 \cdots, n-1 \tag{5.6}$$

If chance is the only factor that affects these differences, then the null hypothesis is given by H_0. There are an equal number of plus and minus $(\Delta k_i - \Delta k_{i+1})$ differences. Under H_0, the probability of getting a positive difference is 0.5.

The probability of getting a particular number of plus signs in N observations can be found by the binomial rule with $p = 0.5$.

Testing Hypothesis #4

To test this hypothesis, it is necessary to have data on items that have been promoted a number of times in the regular season. In addition, each item should preferably have been promoted at a single price in this time period. The items in Departments 2 and 3 do not satisfy these requirements. In fact, there were either no promotions or only a single promotion for about half the items in Department 2 and for all items in Department 3. The other items in Department 2 that were promoted violated the requirement of the promotion taking place at a single price. So only items in Department 1 can be used to test this hypothesis.

Table 5.6 shows the calculations of the signs of the differences in the Δks over time. Note that there are a total of fourteen plus signs out of $N = 19$ observations. When $N > 10$, a normal approximation to the binomial distribution can be used. The proportion of plus differences, P, in the data can be calculated. The hypothesis tested is that the sample with the proportion, P, came from a population with a true proportion of $p = 0.5$. The appropriate statistic in this case is given by:

$$z = \frac{P - p - 1/2N}{\sqrt{p(1 - p)/N}} \tag{5.7}$$

With $P = 14/19$ and $N = 19$, $z = 1.835$.

From the normal distribution, the prob. value is 0.034. This implies that there is a low probability that the difference in the number of plus and minus signs observed could have occurred by chance. Therefore, the conclusion is that there is substantial evidence in support of the fourth hypothesis. It is important to remember that data from only one department were used to test this hypothesis. It is possible that the promotional response during the early life-cycle is different for fashion items in the other departments.

A Regression Model for k

The previous sections investigated some of the major determinants of demand and the nature of their effect on k. However, the magnitude of the effects of these variables on k is still not clear. This section will test a few regression models for k and present some of the results which will given an indication of the magnitude of these effects. Furthermore, the regression equations will be

Table 5.6.   Sign Test for Difference in Δk_i

Item	Δk_i	Sign
2B	0.0771	
	0.0608	+
2C	0.0222	
	0.0409	−
	0.0341	+
	0.0325	+
2D	0.0393	
	0.0504	−
	0.0253	+
2F	0.3267	
	0.4475	−
	0.1328	+
	0.0734	+
2G	0.1401	
	0.1143	+
	0.0824	+
	0.0621	+
2H	0.1914	
	0.0835	+
2I	0.0899	
	0.0489	+
	0.0394	+
	0.0467	−
2J	0.0505	
	0.0743	−
	0.0554	+
	0.0532	+

used as an input to a model for finding the optimal price path that will be developed later.

Aggregate versus Disaggregate Data

Either aggregate data (i.e., total sales and total inventory over all stores) or disaggregate data could be used for this analysis. There are both advantages and disadvantages in these two approaches. These are outlined in table 5.7. The data will be analyzed at both the aggregate and the disaggregate levels.

Variables Used in the Study

The factors affecting k at the aggregate level (that have the same numerical value across all stores) and their measures are given below:

(1)   Time, *T:* This will signify the number of weeks from the time the item is introduced into the store

(2)   Price, *P,* or markup on cost, *M:* Markup allows comparison of the effect of different prices from item to item

(3)   Season: As noted earlier, the Christmas season has a positive effect on *k*. A variable, XMAS, that will be used to represent this effect is shown in figure 5.4. This variable starts to increase seven weeks before the week of Christmas. It is based on the analysis given on page 43

(4)   The absolute inventory level, *I:* A higher inventory (up to a certain limit) may result in better sales due to the breadth effect (better color-size combinations). Furthermore, sales are restricted to be less than the inventory.

Additionally, at the individual store level (disaggregate data), two other factors can be considered. These are floor space, i.e., display area in the store, *F*; and the age of the store, *A*.

Aggregate Model

A number of models were formulated (linear, Cobb-Douglas, exponential, and log-linear) with *k* as the dependent variable and time, markup, XMAS and

Table 5.7.   Comparison of Aggregate versus Disaggregate Data

Disaggregate	Aggregate
A greater degree of noise is inherent in this data	Smoother data: noise at disaggregate level tends to cancel out
Increased cost of collecting and analyzing the larger volume of data	Lower cost of analysis due to smaller volume of data
Errors have a significantly higher effect on the analysis and results	Errors in disaggregate data tend to cancel out. Effect on analysis and results less significant.
Extra information: store specific factors such as store age, floor space, customer profile, etc. can give better insight	Effect of store specific factors are lost when data is aggregated
Parameters could possibly be predicted from large number of data points, at an early stage	Limited data points: early predictions may be difficult

Figure 5.4.   Structure of the XMAS Variable

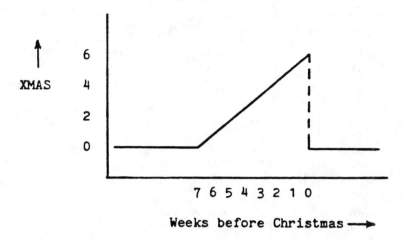

inventory as the independent variables. Both the simple linear model and the Cobb-Douglas model gave pretty high r^2 and significant F values.

Results of the simple linear regression (Equation 5.8) for items in Departments 1 and 2 are given in tables 5.8 and 5.9. A summary of these is given in tables 5.10 and 5.11.

$$k = c_0 + c_1 T + c_2 M + c_3 XMAS + c_4 I \tag{5.8}$$

These results show that for the most part the coefficients of the independent variables had the desired signs. They were negative for markup and time, and positive for inventory and XMAS.

A positive coefficient for inventory suggests the existence of the "breadth" effect. It can be verified that a "hypothetical" staple item (which has constant sales) would have a negative inventory coefficient.

The two departments seem to behave differently with regard to the XMAS variable. This suggests that it may be necessary to have a different basis to fix this variable depending on the historical data for each department.

Disaggregate Model

For the disaggregate model, two more independent variables could be used for each store — age of the store, A, and floor area of the store, F. Here again the simple linear model (Equation 5.9) gave results which were comparable to the results from the more complex models. The results are given in table 5.12.

Table 5.8   Simple Linear Regression on Aggregate Data for Items
in Department 1

Item	c_0	Markup	Time	Inven.	XMAS	r^2	s_e	F
1A	0.223	−1.58	−0.75	1.54	1.62	0.68	0.073	9.11
	(1.13)	(0.18)	(1.79)	(1.54)	(1.97)			
1B	0.286	−9.07	0.58	0.05	0.29	0.57	0.041	4.32
	(1.59)	(2.62)	(0.73)	(0.22)	(0.54)			
1C	0.917	−11.75	−3.18	3.35	0.83	0.77	0.021	10.10
	(2.97)	(4.87)	(2.27)	(2.10)	(3.44)			
1D	1.260	−12.43	−4.96	4.09	3.33	0.72	0.046	6.30
	(3.61)	(2.23)	(3.31)	(2.33)	(2.60)			
1E	0.617	−19.48	−0.97	0.09	−0.92	0.88	0.033	22.8
	(8.12)	(4.82)	(4.85)	(0.91)	(1.85)			
1F	0.021	No Price	−0.74	0.44	1.97	0.66	0.065	8.73
	(0.09)	Variation	(1.62)	(0.58)	(2.22)			
1G	0.440	−5.49	−1.75	0.63	1.68	0.64	0.063	5.00
	(1.52)	(0.45)	(2.33)	(0.60)	(1.83)			
1H	0.436	−16.02	−0.59	0.10	−0.57	0.88	0.023	35.71
	(6.71)	(4.90)	(7.32)	(1.84)	(2.31)			
1I	0.409	−4.79	−0.91	0.68	1.29	0.71	0.053	13.64
	(1.61)	(0.37)	(6.86)	(2.67)	(1.10)			
1K	0.355	−17.25	−0.36	2.03	0.86	0.90	0.018	24.10
	(3.34)	(4.72)	(0.49)	(1.53)	(1.03)			

Note: Multiply inventory coefficient by 0.0001; all other coefficients by 0.01; t values of coefficients are shown parenthetically.

$$k = c_0 + c_1 T + c_2 M + c_3 XMAS + c_4 I + c_5 A + c_6 F \qquad (5.9)$$

It is evident that the disaggregate model gives much lower r^2 compared to the aggregate model. This is to be expected because of the greater degree of dispersion in the former.

The inventory variable has a negative coefficient in the disaggregate model. Although this was surprising at first, the inventory coefficients for the fashion items were not as negative as the coefficient for a hypothetical staple item. This supports the existence of the "breadth" effect for fashion items. The negative coefficient for inventory is also explained by the fact that sales are restricted to be less than the inventory on hand. Therefore, when inventory becomes low, it results in a high k. For example, when inventory = 1, sales could be either 0 or 1. So it is possible to get a maximum value of 1 for k. Obviously, at very low levels of inventory, one has to be careful in the interpretation of k — it cannot be taken to be a measure of the sales performance for the item.

The age coefficient is positive and significant, which implies that older "established" stores have a higher inventory turnover. Floor area does not seem to be significant for most of the items. Since the floor space actually allocated to a department and a particular item is not known, predictions on the effect of this variable on the sales of an item cannot be made.

Table 5.9.   Results of Simple Linear Regression on Aggregate Data
for Items in Department 2

Item	c_0	Markup	Time	Inven.	XMAS	r^2	s_e	F
2B	0.277	−17.58	0.55	0.52	1.38	0.88	0.025	14.75
	(1.07)	(5.32)	(0.37)	(0.76)	(3.40)			
2C	0.289	−12.90	0.14	0.01	1.65	0.68	0.028	11.26
	(3.64)	(3.95)	(1.48)	(0.28)	(5.51)			
2D	0.165	−4.05	0.37	0.09	3.34	0.88	0.040	30.29
	(1.62)	(0.95)	(1.46)	(2.33)	(5.99)			
2F	1.294	−29.51	−3.51	1.52	1.22	0.74	0.086	12.77
	(7.48)	(4.24)	(6.22)	(4.16)	(1.05)			
2G	0.393	−7.25	−1.09	0.22	4.33	0.60	0.074	6.10
	(1.74)	(1.90)	(0.80)	(0.32)	(2.58)			
2H	0.221	−8.45	−0.15	0.13	1.81	0.26	0.097	1.49
	(0.53)	(1.21)	(0.08)	(0.12)	(1.29)			
2J	0.305	−16.13	−0.17	1.02		0.97	0.016	76.02
	(4.45)	(7.53)	(0.53)	(5.48)				

(1) Multiply Inventory coefficient by 0.0001; all other coefficients by 0.01

(2) Item 2J was marked down during Xmas and the prices were not known

Table 5.10.   Range of r^2 and Coefficients

	Department #1 (10 Items)	Department #2 (7 Items)
r^2	+0.57 to +0.90	+0.26 to +0.97
Markup	−0.016 to −0.195	−0.041 to −0.295
Time	−0.050 to +0.006[a]	−0.035 to +0.006[b]
Inven.	+0.050 to +4.090	+0.010 to +1.520
Xmas	−0.009 to +0.033[c]	+0.012 to +0.043

a = > 1 positive coefficient in range
b = > 3 positive coefficients in range
c = > 3 negative coefficients in range

Table 5.11.   Number of Significant Variables at the 95% Confidence Level and the Signs of Their Coefficients

	Department #1 (10 Items)	Department #2 (7 Items)
Markup	6 −	6 −
Time	6 −	2 −
Inven.	4 +	2 +
Xmas	5 + & 2 −	5 +

Table 5.12. Results of Simple Linear Regression on Disaggregate Data

Item	c_0	Markup	Time	Inven.	Xmas	Age	Floor	r^2	s_e	F
1C	0.183 (4.88)	−0.01 (3.14)	−0.03 (2.19)	−0.07 (7.85)	−0.05 (2.42)	0.03 (2.51)	7.00 (1.96)	0.10	0.168	18.62
1D	0.286 (8.30)	−0.74 (5.53)	−0.05 (2.96)	−0.03 (7.09)	−0.15 (5.80)	0.02 (2.46)	0.40 (0.13)	0.19	0.130	35.92
2D	0.235 (7.27)	−1.40 (8.77)	0.03 (2.97)	−0.00 (5.00)	0.28 (13.43)	0.02 (2.47)	−3.20 (1.37)	0.36	0.117	114.17
2F	0.647 (17.37)	−2.80 (14.45)	−0.24 (19.52)	−0.03 (7.13)	0.23 (7.99)	0.03 (3.90)	−1.00 (0.30)	0.25	0.174	76.42
2I	0.459 (11.70)	−2.69 (11.40)	−0.10 (7.90)	−0.02 (12.60)	0.35 (6.10)	0.00 (0.02)	−1.80 (0.20)	0.22	0.155	55.21
4D	0.570 (9.50)	−0.02 (9.60)	−0.02 (1.30)	−0.02 (6.70)	0.42 (17.70)	0.07 (7.20)	1.40 (0.44)	0.48	0.135	135.60
4I	0.500 (8.10)	−0.02 (7.70)	−0.05 (2.26)	−0.02 (4.34)	0.17 (7.98)	0.06 (5.15)	0.10 (0.02)	0.25	0.131	40.40

Multiply floor coefficient by 0.0001; all other coefficients by 0.01

6

Pricing Models

This chapter develops two models that deal with the pricing problem for fashion items. It has already been established that the inherent demand for fashion items decreases over time. Under these circumstances, the decision-maker will have to take some action to improve the sales performance of the item. The most direct mechanism to achieve this is price reduction.

The first model that will be developed can be looked upon as a satisficing model. It can be used by the manager both to evaluate the current performance of an item and to aid him in deciding if the item should be marked down (and if so, by how much). The second model is an optimizing model. It specifies the optimal price path of an item over time given the demand function for the item. It can therefore be used as a planning tool.

A Simple Markdown Model

The scenario is as follows: The manager (buyer) feels that a fashion item is currently not performing well. This could be due to any number of reasons, including high initial markup, natural decline in sales, bad timing, and broken color-size assortment. The manager wants to discover if reducing the price would prove worthwhile. To analyze this problem, it is necessary to define the following variables:

p Current selling price
d Markdown price (decision variable)
w_p Average number of weeks to sell a "dog" (i.e., an item not selling well) at the current price, p
w_d Average number of weeks to sell a "dog" at the markdown price, d
K Average turnover of good stock for the line (which has similar items) or for the entire department. This is the average (sales/inventory) ratio
m Markup on cost (dollar markup/dollar cost)

Assume that all the variables except d (and w_d, which is a function of d) are known or can be estimated. Consider one unit of the "dog." The manager has two alternatives: he can continue selling the item at \$ p and take an average of w_p weeks to sell it; or he can take a markdown on the item and sell it for \$ d, thereby taking an average of w_d weeks to dispose of the item ($w_d < w_p$).

Consider the same time period as the basis for comparing these two alternatives. In this case, the longer time period, w_p, will be used as the basis for comparison. If the item is marked down, the manager gets to make use of the revenues generated in the w_d weeks, for ($w_p - w_d$) weeks. Presumably, this revenue would be invested in getting new items that have an average turnover ratio of K per week and an average gross margin of m. The new items will turn over $K(w_p - w_d)$ times in this period. Therefore, the total margin generated will be \$ $dmK(w_p - w_d)$.

It is worthwhile to take a markdown only if the total return from this alternative equals or exceeds the revenue from selling it at its regular price. In this formulation the discount rate is assumed to be zero. This assumption is not very critical to the model, considering its short time frame (a few weeks). Therefore,

$$p \leqslant d + d\, m\, K\, (w_p - w_d) \tag{6.1}$$

There are two unknowns in this equation: d and w_d (which is a function of d). This equation can be explicitly solved for the value of d. Assuming some value for the markdown price, d, an estimate can be obtained for the value of w_d. This is used in Equation 6.1 to see if the expected revenue from the markdown is greater than p. This calculation must be done for different values of d after which the markdown price that gives the highest revenue is chosen.

Implementation

The success or failure of this model hinges on obtaining the values of w_p and w_d. One way to get estimates for these variables is using the Decision Calculus approach pioneered by Little [22]. This involves asking the managers for a few estimates of these variables and constructing a response curve. This response curve is then used as an input to the model. This approach has a number of advantages, the most important being user-acceptance, since the users (managers) feel that they are in control of the decision-making process.

A second approach is to use the information presented in the last chapter on the determinants and structure of demand. It has been established that k is a decreasing function of time in the regular season. As the item becomes older, the absolute reduction in k is expected to become smaller. For example, consider k to have a value of 0.2 when the item is introduced and suppose k drops to 0.03 after 10 weeks, both evaluated at the same price, p. The maximum possible reduction in k at these two points in time are 0.2 and 0.03 respectively (because the minimum possible value for k is zero). As a result k should be decreasing at a slower rate. Therefore, as the item gets older it should be possible to get better estimates of the future k's based on the current value of k, since the predictive range is smaller (0 to 0.03 in our example). The lower limit of w_p is $(1/k)$, since k is decreasing over time.

Predicting w_d on the other hand is a more difficult task. If the item has been sold at a number of different price levels, it is possible to get some idea of its price elasticity. If not, w_d will have to be based on the experience and judgment of the buyer.

Discussion

This model can be classified as a satisficing model, because there is no attempt made to find the optimal solution. Its main virtue lies in its simplicity. Since some of the parameters of the model are based upon the judgment of the user, the results of the model are to a certain degree sensitive to the perceptions of the person who uses the model.

A nice feature of this model is its ability to handle the concepts of price points and psychological pricing. All that has to be done is to restrict the value of the markdown price, d, to a discrete set of values corresponding to these price points.

The model does not predict the point in time at which it would be worthwhile to take a markdown, nor does it provide the length of time that a given price should be in effect. This is its biggest drawback, as it has to be used on a regular basis by the manager to determine whether or not a markdown should be taken.

A Control Theory Model

This section develops a more complex model than the one in the previous section. This model addresses the general pricing problem for fashion items over time. It was formulated in a control theoretical framework and is an optimizing model.

The model ignores the effect of special events such as Christmas on the demand for the item. On the basis of the statistical work presented in the previous chapter, k is assumed to be a decreasing function of time. The question, then, is to find the point in time at which the price reduction should be considered, and to determine the magnitude of this reduction.

What are the factors that will affect the timing and magnitude of the price reduction? A very important factor is the regular retail price of the item. If this is too high then the item will sell slowly (i.e., it will have a low k), and a price reduction will be required. Finding the "optimal" initial markup for the item is outside the scope of this work; it will be assumed that this is either known or given. The buyers fix the initial markup for an item based on their experience and knowledge of the competition, vendors, market conditions, and management guidelines and philosophy. Another important factor which will affect the magnitude of the price reduction is the rate of decline of k.

With this background, the general characteristics of the pricing problem for fashion items is to determine the optimal pricing path over time, given a certain stock of the fashion item. In actual practice, the prices will be changed at discrete time intervals (for example, on a weekly basis). However, a continuous time formulation and solution could provide some insight into the nature of the discrete time problem. A discrete time formulation, such as dynamic programming, could be computationally infeasible for very large problems (when there are many weeks and/or many price levels). For these reasons, the problem will be formulated using a control theory framework and it will be solved for certain special cases.

General Formulation

Assume that there is some beginning inventory. There is a certain time span, T, needed to clear this inventory from the shop floor. The control variable is the price which is a function of time, $p(t)$, and the performance index is the discounted revenue from time 0 to time T. The terminal condition is the salvage value of the item at time T, which will be denoted at p_s. It is assumed that the salvage value is independent of the quantity left over at time T. The governing equation is:

$$s(t) \ = \ k \cdot I(t) \tag{6.2}$$

This is the definition of k (the sales to inventory ratio) in a continuous time framework. The sales rate is equal to the negative of the rate of change of inventory.

$$s(t) \ = \ - \ \frac{dI(t)}{dt} \tag{6.3}$$

The revenue at any time, t, is:

$$R(t) \ = \ p(t) \cdot s(t) \ = \ k \cdot p(t) \cdot I(t) \tag{6.4}$$

In the simplest case, k is taken to be a function of time and price. This defines the response function (i.e., how the demand for the item changes over time and responds to price changes).

$$k = k(p(t),t) \tag{6.5}$$

Assume that there is no constraint on the selling price of the item at any point in time. The discounted revenue has to be maximized with respect to the control variable $p(t)$.

With a discount rate of r, this can be written as:

$$\text{Max } p(t) \int_0^T p(t) \cdot k(p(t),t) \cdot I(t) \cdot \exp(-rt)\, dt$$

$$+ p_s \cdot I(T) \cdot \exp(-rT) \tag{6.6}$$

subject to

$$\frac{d\,I(t)}{dt} = -k(p(t),t)\, I(t) \tag{6.7}$$

$$p(t) \geqslant p_s \exp\left[-r(T-t)\right] \tag{6.8}$$

The first term in the revenue function is the discounted revenue from sales of the item from time 0 to T, at price $p(t)$. The second term is the terminal condition which is the discounted revenue from selling the inventory left over at the end of time T, $I(T)$, at the salvage value p_s. The first constraint in the model is the driving equation. The second constraint implies that if $p(t)$ is less than the discounted salvage value, it is worthwhile to hold the item until time T and sell it at the salvage value. To solve this problem, define the Hamiltonian function, H, with $\lambda(t)$ as the adjoint variable.

$$H = p(t)\, k(p(t),t)\, I(t) \exp(-rt) - \lambda(t)\, k(p,t)\, I(t) \tag{6.9}$$

Denote the partial derivatives with respect to time by a $(\cdot)$ over the function. The sufficient conditions for the optimal price path are given by Equations 6.10, 6.11, and 6.12.

$$\frac{\partial H}{\partial p} = k(p(t),t)\, I(t) \exp(-rt) + p(t)\, I(t) \exp(-rt)\, \frac{\partial k}{\partial p}$$

$$- \lambda(t)\, I(t)\, \frac{\partial k}{\partial p} = 0 \tag{6.10}$$

The adjoint equation is given by

$$\frac{\partial H}{\partial I} = p(t)\, k(p,t) \exp(-rt) - \lambda(t)\, k(p,t) = -\dot{\lambda}(t) \tag{6.11}$$

The terminal condition is given by

$$\lambda(T) = \frac{\partial (p_s I(T) \exp(-rT))}{\partial I(T)} = p_s \exp(-rT) \tag{6.12}$$

This system of equations can be manipulated to give a differential equation in λ. This differential equation can be solved, knowing the terminal condition. Equation 6.9 can then be used to solve explicitly for $p(t)$ in terms of $\lambda(t)$, which gives the optimal price path from time 0 to T.

In the case of a constraint on price, there is a limitation on the maximum price that can be charged for the item, i.e.,

$$p(t) < p_m \quad \text{for all } t \tag{6.13}$$

where p_m is the maximum price that can be charged. The salvage value of the item is p_s. The problem is to find the optimal price path under these constraints.

The model that was presented in the previous section will basically be the same when there is a price constraint. The Hamiltonian will be modified slightly to reflect the new constraint, and is given by

$$H' = H + \mu (p(t) - p_m) \tag{6.14}$$

The multiplier μ is such that

$$\mu \geq 0 \text{ for } p = p_m, \mu = 0 \text{ for } p \leq p_m \tag{6.15}$$

This will modify Equation 6.10 and, consequently, the optimal price path.

Linear Response Function

Assume the following functional form for k:

$$k(p,t) = k_0 - \beta p - \gamma t \geq 0 \tag{6.16}$$

This is the simplest model for k, which makes it a decreasing function of time and price. k is restricted to be nonnegative so that sales would be nonnegative. Substituting this function in Equation 6.10 gives $p(t)$ in terms of $\lambda(t)$.

$$p(t) = 0.5\,[\,\lambda \exp(-rt) + \beta^{-1})\,(k_0 - \gamma t)]\tag{6.17}$$

Using Equations 6.16 and 6.17, $p(t)$ and $k(t)$ can be eliminated from Equation 6.11 to give a differential equation in λ.

$$\dot{\lambda} + \lambda^2\,(0.25\,\beta \exp(rt)) - 0.5\,\lambda\,(k_0 - \gamma t) + \frac{(k_0 - \gamma t)^2}{4\,\beta \exp(rt)} = 0\tag{6.18}$$

This is a first-order nonlinear Riccati equation. It can be simplified by using the following transformation:

$$m(t) = \lambda(t) - \frac{(k_0 - \gamma t)}{\beta \exp(rt)}\tag{6.19}$$

This results in a Riccati equation in terms of the variable $m(t)$.

$$\dot{m} + m^2 f(t) - g(t) = 0\tag{6.20}$$

where $f(t) = 0.25\,\beta \exp(rt)$, $g(t) = (r(k_0 - \gamma t) + \gamma)\beta \exp(rt)$. Equation 6.20 can be changed into a simpler second order differential equation by the following transformation:

$$u(t) = \exp[\int_0^t f(t)m(t)dt]\tag{6.21}$$

This results in

$$\ddot{u} - r\dot{u} - [0.25\,(r\,(k_0 - \gamma t) + \gamma)]\,u = 0\tag{6.22}$$

It is difficult to obtain explicit solutions for Equation 6.22 for all values of r. The solution in the general case when $r = 0$ can be found in the literature. (For example, see Murray [25].) However, it is given in terms of Bessel functions, which makes it unwieldy and messy to calculate.) The special case when $r = 0$ will also be considered here. This simplifies Equation 6.22 to

$$\ddot{u} - 0.25\,\gamma u = 0\tag{6.24}$$

The solution for this equation is given by

$$u(t) = c_1 \exp(Dt) + c_2 \exp(-Dt) \tag{6.25}$$

where c_1 and c_2 are the constants of integration and D is given by

$$D = 0.5\gamma^{0.5} \tag{6.26}$$

Case 1: Price unconstrained. The two constants can be solved by the boundary condition from Equation 6.12, and from the transformations. It is given by

$$\frac{\dot{u}(T)}{u(T)} = f(T)\, m(T)$$

$$= f(T)\,[\lambda(T) - \beta \exp(-rT)\,(k_0 - \gamma t)] \tag{6.27}$$

The constants are

$$c_1 = (D + \vartheta)\,\frac{\exp(-DT)}{(D + \vartheta)\exp(-DT) + (D - \vartheta)\exp(DT)} \tag{6.28}$$

$$c_2 = 1 - c_1 \tag{6.29}$$

where ϑ is given by

$$\vartheta = 0.25\,(\beta p_s - k_0 + \gamma T) \tag{6.30}$$

$p(t)$ can now be obtained from the inverse transforms — i.e., $m(t)$ can be found from $u(t)$, $\lambda(t)$ from $m(t)$, and $p(t)$ from $\lambda(t)$. The optimal price path is then given by

$$p(t) = Q(t) \text{ for } Q(t) \geqslant p_s$$

$$= p_s \text{ for } Q(t) < p_s \tag{6.31}$$

where

$$Q(t) = \frac{2D}{\beta}\,\frac{c_1 \exp(Dt) - c_2 \exp(-Dt)}{c_1 \exp(Dt) + c_2 \exp(-Dt)} + \frac{(k_0 - \gamma t)}{\beta} \tag{6.32}$$

The constants D, c_1, c_2 in Equation 6.32 are defined by Equations 6.26, 6.28, and 6.29 respectively.

Case 2: Constraint on price. With the simple price constraint formulated (Equation 6.13), the entire problem does not have to be re-solved. From Equation 6.15 it can be seen that μ will be 0 when the price constraint is not tight. Therefore, the time t' at which the price constraint just becomes nonbinding can be found. It is given by the following equation:

$$(p_m \beta - k_0) = \frac{c_1 \exp(Dt') - c_2 \exp(-Dt')}{c_1 \exp(Dt') + c_2 \exp(-Dt')} \gamma^{0.5} - \gamma t' \qquad (6.33)$$

The optimal price path is that in which the price charged will be p_m from time 0 to t'. After that point it will follow the price path found in the discussion of the unconstrained case.

Calculation Procedure

The optimal pricing policy can be calculated quite easily by using numerical methods. An example of this is shown in figures 6.1 and 6.2 for sample values of the parameters β and γ. The following values were used for the other variables: time $T = 20$, $k_0 = 0.9$, and salvage value $p_s = 5$.

These plots show that price is a decreasing function of time for any given combination of parameters. However, the price path may not be a monotonic function over the parameters β and γ, as is evident in figure 6.2. This is a result of the interaction of price and the sales rate. There is a trade-off involved in reducing the price quickly in order to increase the sales rate. The revenue which is the product of the price and sales rate could therefore be adversely affected if the price were reduced at a rate faster than the optimal rate of decrease.

The total revenue for the price paths obtained can be calculated. The revenues are calculated for a beginning inventory, $I_0 = 100$. The results of these calculations are shown in tables 6.1 and 6.2 for both the unconstrained price (Case 1), and the constrained price (Case 2: $p \leq 20$) situations. These revenues are not calculated on the basis of continuous price change over the entire time period. The price at the beginning of a week is assumed to be held constant over the week, which results in a step function for price changes over time. In general, the unconstrained price revenue should be greater than the constrained price revenue. This is evident in the results shown in table 6.2. However, in some cases the revenue with a price constraint is higher than the revenue without a price constraint. This is because the continuous price path resulting from the model was approximated as a step function for price over time. The differences between the two are not significant.

It is evident that as the values of the parameters β and γ increase, the revenue decreases. Furthermore, the difference in the revenue between the two cases also decreases as these parameters increase. This result is to be expected,

Figure 6.1. Optimal Pricing Policy (Case 1: Price Unconstrained)

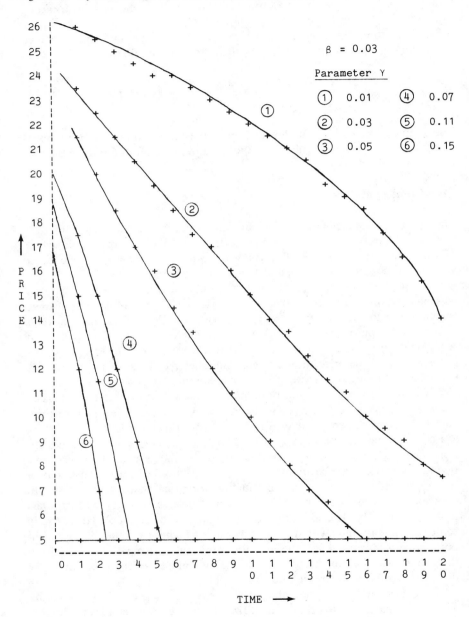

Figure 6.2. Optimal Pricing Policy (Case 2 : Price Constrained)

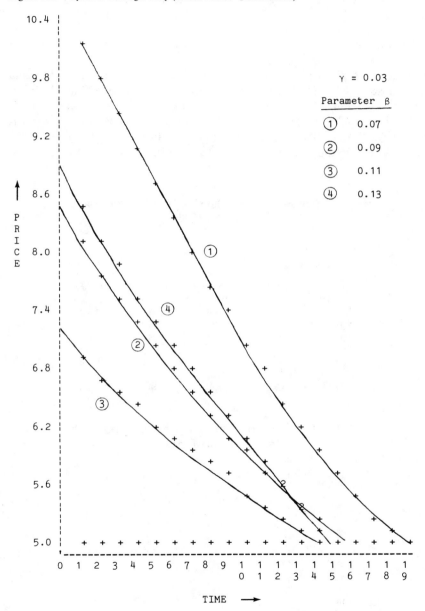

since increasing these parameters implies that k (and thus the sales rate) decreases.

Implementation

The basic inputs required for this model are the coefficients of the variables in the response function for k. Regression analysis can be used to find the values of these coefficients. The buyers generally bring in new merchandise for the upcoming season and dispose of the old merchandise by taking markdowns just after Christmas. The response function used in the example given in the previous section is appropriate for the "after Christmas" period. As mentioned

Table 6.1.   Revenues from Following Optimal Price Path
from Control Model

| | $\gamma = 0.03$ | | $\gamma = 0.10$ | |
β	Case 1	Case 2	Case 1	Case 2
0.01	5857	2000	3937	1962
0.03	1963	1872	1358	1362
0.05	1188	1188	855	858
0.07	861	861	652	656
0.09	688	688	554	559
0.11	584	584	509	515
0.13	500	500	500	500

Table 6.2.   Revenues from Following Optimal Price Path
from Control Model

| | $\beta = 0.03$ | | $\beta = 0.10$ | |
γ	Case 1	Case 2	Case 1	Case 2
0.01	2299	1989	710	710
0.03	1963	1872	631	631
0.05	1735	1706	554	557
0.07	1482	1483	545	556
0.09	1407	1421	530	531
0.11	1313	1331	522	536
0.13	1229	1264	514	521
0.15	1166	1180	505	507
0.17	1099	1156	500	500

earlier, the retail price is assumed to be given. This corresponds to having a constraint on price. The procedure to implement this model is given in figure 6.3.

The decision to change the price for an item will depend on the standard error of the regression for k. If there is a large variance in the system resulting in a large confidence interval for k, then it might be better to wait for a "better" signal (and take into account other factors) before changing prices.

Better estimates for the values of the coefficients of the independent variables could be obtained as more data is collected over time. Therefore, the price path for an item suggested by the model will evolve over time. This is advantageous from a competitive standpoint, since it will make it much more difficult for the competition to figure out the exact pricing policy.

From a practical viewpoint it would not be feasible to have a continuous change in the price of the items. It is therefore necessary to change price at certain convenient time periods. The model could still be used as a very good approximation of the discrete time interval problem. If the retailer decides that it is necessary to have a certain number of price points, the graphs can be used to determine the optimal time at which the price change should be made. In other words, fixing the price fixes the time period at which this price should be changed.

The concepts of discrete "price points" and psychological pricing have not been considered here because the model assumes a continuous response function (k as a function of price and time). It would be difficult to handle these concepts in the control theory framework because the response functions would have to be discontinuous. Solving the differential equations to get explicit equation(s) for the optimal price path when the response functions are nonlinear is cumbersome. The effect of special events such as Christmas, which have a positive impact on k, have also not been considered.

A Demonstration

The control theory model will be tested by applying it to a few items in Department 1. The first step is to obtain the coefficients of price and time in the response function for k. The data from the time the item was introduced to the beginning of the Christmas season (November 3) will be used for this purpose. Because the value of the price coefficient is required, the item should have been sold at a minimum of two different prices in this period.

The simple linear regressions gave the following response functions:

$$1A : k = 0.838 - 0.0467 \,(\text{PRICE}) - 0.020 \,(\text{TIME})$$

$$1D : k = 0.430 - 0.0229 \,(\text{PRICE}) - 0.010 \,(\text{TIME})$$

Figure 6.3. Procedure to Implement Control Model

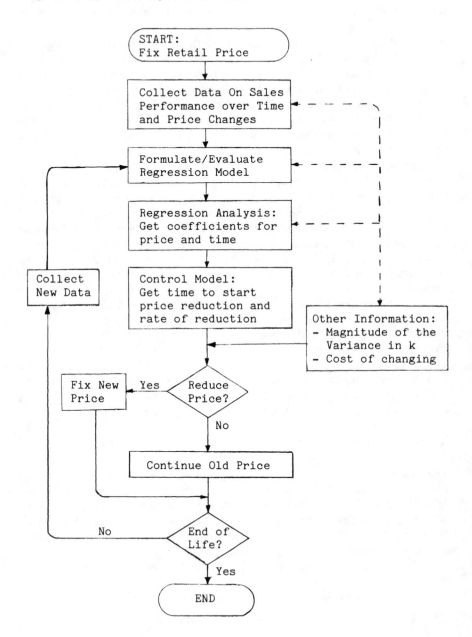

1E : k = 0.860 − 0.0467 (PRICE) − 0.003 (TIME)

1H : k = 0.635 − 0.0350 (PRICE) − 0.006 (TIME)

The inputs to the model were the coefficients of price and time, the estimated life of the item, and the estimated salvage value.

The items were assumed to have a life span of fifteen weeks and an estimated salvage value of one third of the retail price of the item. The optimal price path for the four items are shown in figures 6.4 to 6.7. As can be seen from the graphs, if the price is made to be less than or equal to the retail price of the item as determined by the buyer, the model says that the price has to be reduced at the time schedule given in the table shown below.

Item	Weeks after Introduction
1A	8
1D	6
1E	7
1H	6

The optimal price path for the items shows that without a price constraint, the starting prices are not very different from the retail prices actually set by the buyers. The recommended rate for the price reduction is different for the four items and is a function of the values of the coefficients for price and time for each of the items.

Effect of the Size of Ending Inventory

Until now, the salvage value, p_s, has been assumed to be independent of the size of the ending inventory, I_T. What will be the effect of relaxing this assumption on the optimal price path dictated by the control model?

Realistically, p_s can be expected to be an inverse function of I_T, i.e., if there is a huge volume of inventory at the end of the season (time T), the salvage price recovered per item would be low. Assume that a schedule of the relationship between p_s and I_T is given. This could either be in the form of a table or in the form of an algebraic function. As a starting point, assume some value for p_s (for example, p_s = 0). The control model can be applied to give the optimal price path, and hence I_T (given a starting inventory, I_0). If I_T from the model corresponds to the assumed p_s, the solution has been obtained. If not, assume a new value for p_s (which could be the value corresponding to I_T obtained earlier), and apply the control model again. This iterative procedure should be continued until I_T and p_s correspond. This procedure results in an

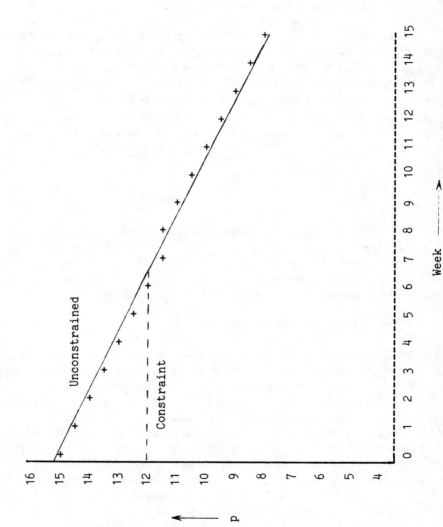

Figure 6.4.   Optimal Price Path for Item 1A

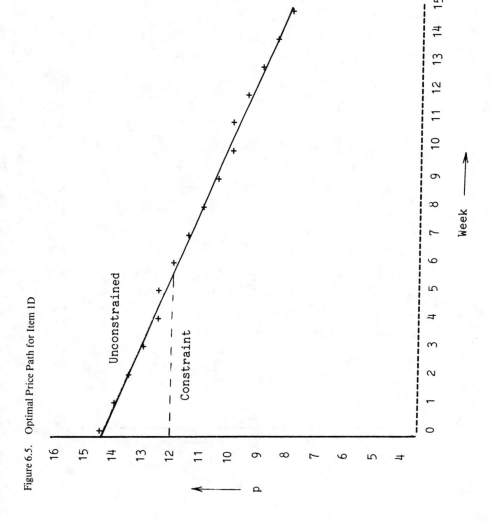

Figure 6.5.   Optimal Price Path for Item 1D

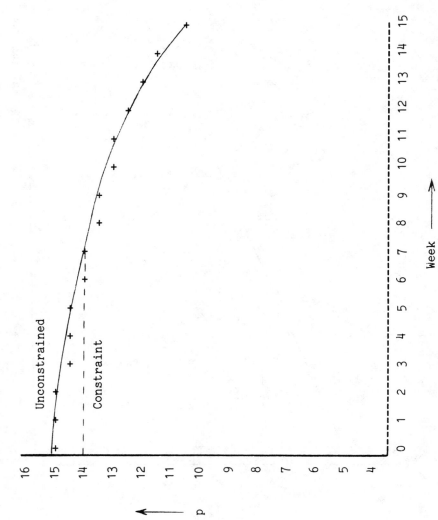

Figure 6.6.   Optimal Price Path for Item 1E

Figure 6.7. Optimal Price Path for Item 1H

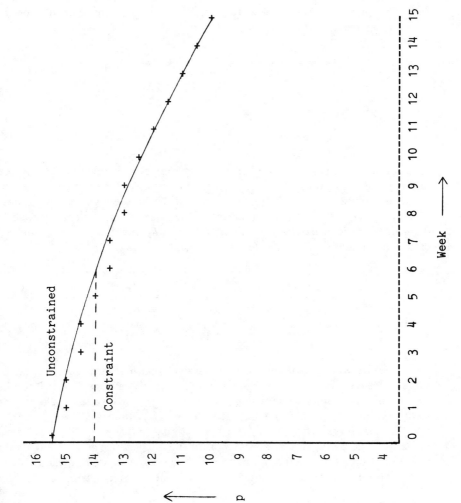

optimal price path which will be a function of the beginning inventory. Figure 6.8 provides a flowchart of this procedure.

If the relationship between p_s and I_T is an algebraic function, an infinite number of iterations may be needed, in theory, to obtain a solution. In that case, it is necessary to specify limits on the correspondence between p_s and I_T so as to stop the iterative process after a finite number of iterations.

This procedure was applied to Item 1A. The following schedule for the relationship between p_s and I_T was assumed.

Ending Inventory, I_T	Salvage Value, p_s
0 - 100	4.0
101 - 200	3.5
201 - 300	3.0
301 - 400	2.4
401 - 600	2.0

The following values for the other variables were also assumed: $I_0 = 10,000$ units; $p_s = \$4.0$; time, $T = 15$ weeks. The response function for k was the same as the one given in the previous section. Using these values, three iterations were required to reach equilibrium. The price paths specified by each of the three iterations are shown in figure 6.9. The I_T (obtained from the model) and p_s (assumed) for the three iterations are shown below.

Iteration	p_s	I_T
1	4.0	504
2	2.0	381
3	2.4	403

Another way to look at this problem is to realize that as I_0 is increased, larger price reductions are required. A large I_0 will give a large I_T which results in a smaller per unit salvage value. Therefore, it is worthwhile to take higher reductions and try to sell more units of the item before time T.

The relationship between I_T and p_s is external to the model. This will have to be specified by the buyers on the basis of their experience and/or judgment. It could also be estimated from historical data on the average salvage dollars realized for a given level of ending inventory for items in a department.

Effect of the Christmas Season

The effect of the Christmas season was not included in the control model, as this would make the model very complex. Although no attempt will be made to solve this problem, it remains a worthwhile issue to examine. It could provide some guidelines for fashion merchandising managers and also lay the ground-work for future research in this ara.

There are three possibilities if the control model were applied before the beginning of the Christmas season. The model may prescribe a decline in price starting either before the start of the Christmas season, or during the Christmas season, or after the end of the Christmas season. The first two possibilities create problems. It is known that the Christmas season has a positive impact on k. Therefore, the dollar value of inventory at the beginning of the Christmas season should be higher than the one implicitly calculated in the control model. To overcome this problem it is necessary to estimate the "real dollar worth" of the inventory at the start of the Christmas season.

This estimate could be based on an average (or expected) k during the Christmas season and the estimated salvage value of the item at the end of the Christmas season. Getting these values is crucial; once these values are obtained, the control model could be rerun to get the price path before the beginning of the Christmas season.

A DSS Framework

The successful implementation of the control model will require a good infra-structure to capture, store, and maintain transaction data. The buyers cannot be expected to conduct the regression analysis and run the control model. Therefore, it will be necessary to make this procedure a part of a Decision Support System (DSS). This requires the development of software packages that will require the buyers to do a minimum of data manipulation, allow them to modify any of the parameters on the basis of their judgment and/or experience, and give them a suggested price plan as an output. This DSS frame-work is depicted in figures 6.10 and 6.11.

Some General Comments on the Models

One cost which has not been considered in this analysis is that of changing the prices of the items. This cost would depend on the policy of the store and their merchandise control system. In some organizations, the prices in the data base and the price signs on the shelves or racks are the only places where the changes have to be made. In such cases there is only a fixed cost involved in changing prices. In other organizations, the price tag on every item is changed. This involves both a fixed cost and a variable cost component for labor depending on the number of price tags that have to be changed. This cost will also affect the rate of change of price over time.

An effect of reducing prices, which has not been accounted for in both the models, is the extra customer traffic (and extra revenue) which is generated

Figure 6.8.   Iterative Procedure When Salvage Value Is a Known Function
             of Ending Inventory

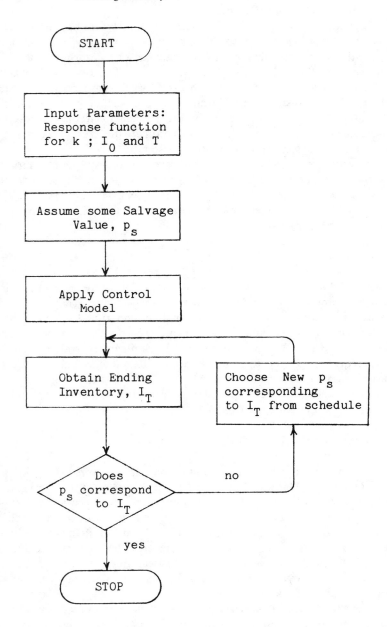

Figure 6.9. Price Path from the Iterative Procedure for Item 1A

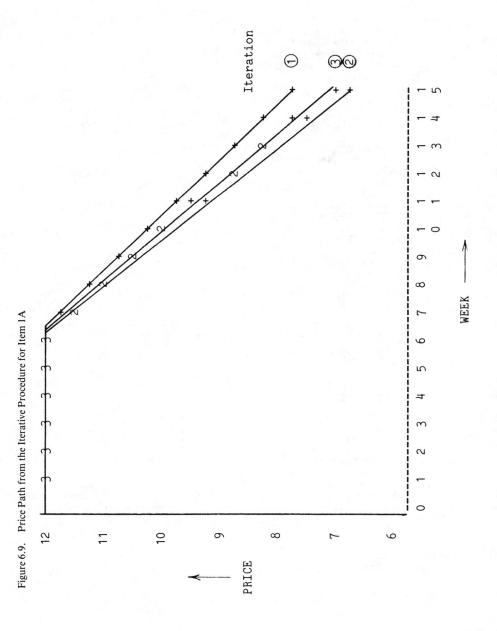

Figure 6.10.   A DSS Framework to Implement Control Model

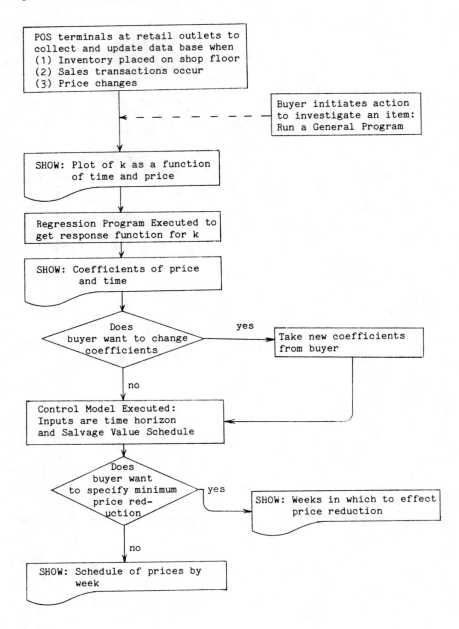

Figure 6.11. User Interaction in the DSS

```
RUN PROGRAM

INPUT ITEM NAME  :  1A

                ┌─────────────────────────────────────┐
                │ DISPLAY:                            │
                │                                     │
                │ PLOT OF k VS. TIME and PRICE        │
                ├─────────────────────────────────────┤
                │ DISPLAY:                            │
                │                                     │
                │ TIME COEFFICIENT   = -0.0200        │
                │ PRICE COEFFICIENT = -0.0467         │
                └─────────────────────────────────────┘

DO YOU WANT TO CHANGE ANY COEFFICIENT (YES/NO)  :  NO

NUMBER OF WEEKS  :  15

                ┌───────────────────────────────────────┐
                │ DISPLAY:                              │
                │                                       │
                │ SALVAGE VALUE    ENDING INVENTORY     │
                │      ..                ..             │
                │      ..                ..             │
                │      ..                ..             │
                └───────────────────────────────────────┘

DO YOU WANT TO CHANGE SALVAGE VALUE (YES/NO)  :  NO

IS THERE A MINIMUM PRICE REDUCTION THAT YOU DESIRE (YES/NO)  :  NO

                ┌─────────────────────────────┐
                │ DISPLAY:                    │
                │                             │
                │   WEEK        PRICE         │
                │                             │
                │     1          16           │
                │     2          16           │
                │     .          ..           │
                │     .          ..           │
                │    15           8           │
                └─────────────────────────────┘

END OF RUN
```

when there is a "sale" event. This cross-elasticity factor will obviously favor a price reduction.

A limitation of both models is that they do not address the problem of the initial order quantity and replenishments. The concept of k could help the manager in his or her replenishment decisions. If the rate of decline in k is small and the absolute value of k is high with respect to the average k (for this line of merchandise or department) then — depending on the inventory on hand — a reorder might be considered.

7

Conclusions

The research presented in this monograph can be divided into three main categories. First, this study has engendered an understanding of the dynamics of the demand process for fashion nonperishable items. Prior to this research, there had been virtually no systematic empirical investigation of the demand structure for fashion items at the retail level. The present study has also provided an in-depth examination of the institutional structure for the retailing of fashion items. The information contained here should be very useful in managing the life cycle of a fashion item. The Cyert study [10] is the only other literature related to this area. Finally, this research has developed a control theory model to solve the problem of the pricing of a fashion item over time. This model could be used by the buyer as a planning tool.

The Demand Structure: A Summary

The study of the demand for fashion items aimed to establish a framework for developing and testing meaningful hypotheses about the demand structure. The theory was derived from assortment concepts in general retail use for some period of time, and was extended to consider the effect of assortment structure upon the rate of weekly product turnover, a variable given the name of k by Wolfe [39]. This extension is important because the comparison of weekly turnover rates provides a better basis both for viewing the effects of assortment change and for developing inventory control models. Wolfe's empirical work tested the existence of a constant k during the fashion season.

The application of assortment theory to the determinants of k indicated, however, a contrary view. The regular depletion of assortments across a season would generally be expected to diminish their attraction to consumers. This would occur because the residual items in inventories subject to limited or no replenishment would be less likely to meet customer needs. Product turnover rates from broken assortments, therefore, could be expected to be less than that of complete assortments even if both contained the same number of units.

The extension of this view to the impact of price promotions upon k led to the conclusion that these would also decline during the season. Both patterns, however, were expected to be altered by general seasonal trends in demand, such as those existing during the Christmas season.

Drawing upon data derived from the operations of a large retail chain selling primarily soft goods, it was found that k generally declines across an off-holiday seasonal period. However, this pattern was not followed by all classes examined. Items from women's accessories enjoyed relatively stable sales and improved weekly turnover. This proved contrary to both Wolfe's and the present author's views.

Study of the Christmas season upon k showed a strong and positive impact. This occurred in all the departments despite the generally deteriorating quality of assortments that resulted during this period of time.

These findings mirror (in some ways) the difficulties that confront merchants of fashion merchandise. Judging from the data, it is probable that a generally declining k cannot be characteristic of fashion items. While many assortments appear likely to follow such a pattern, deviations are no doubt important and require separate evaluation. What does seem clear, however, is that presumptions about stable k rates across a fashion season are incorrect; and their use in sales estimation models will usually result in the overestimation of the rate of depletion.

The indication that the role of price promotion will generally decline during the season provides initial empirical support for heuristics typically used in the retail trade with respect to markdowns. Where product movement is not satisfactory, the long-held view is that markdowns should be taken early in the season. The data in this study indicate that similar price promotions are less effective in later parts of the season than they are in the beginning.

The findings also indicate that general shifts in exogenous demand will have a major impact upon change in k over time. During the Christmas season, k improved consistently before breaking sharply at the end of December. The role of the declining quality of the assortment, no doubt present, is evidently of lesser significance during this period of time. This suggests cause for caution in interpreting the results, and the need for an examination of the two phenomena as separate effects. Attempts to accomplish this by cross-sectional comparison across stores during each time period were not successful in this regard because of the pervasive store effect on k turnovers.

While additional tests of the k patterns across other time periods and different products should add valuable information to the understanding of the process at work, better measures of assortment quality would also aid immeasurably. The concept of "broken" or unbalanced assortments and the development of the present conceptual framework associated with this appears to have considerable theoretical and empirical relevance. However, empirical evaluation would be greatly improved if indices of assortment deterioration could be derived. This would provide means for ascertaining the relative role of breadth, depth, and exposure to assortment attractiveness.

Since consumer-demand rigidities play a role in assortment, it would be useful to conduct empirical studies in conjunction with studies of consumer preferences. The derivations of mechanisms to contrast the degree of this phenomenon across different product types would be extraordinarily valuable for understanding and predicting sales rates from fashion inventories.

Institutional Structure: A Summary

Although the following observations are based on the study of a specific organization, they are generally applicable to most organizations in the same business.

The organization studied here should improve its management information system. First, it needs to improve its data collection network, especially with regard to the accuracy of data capture. There is a lot of potentially useful information in the initial sales and inventory data on a fashion item once the item is introduced in the stores, provided the data is accurate. Currently, there is no way for the buyer to determine if a shipment has actually been placed on the shop floor unless he or she actually contacts the stores. All that is required to solve this problem is the establishment of a computer terminal (connected to the central data base) at the receiving area in each store. The data base can then be updated as soon as a shipment is actually placed in the selling area.

This system has an added advantage in that it will also serve as a control on the merchandise delivery system and on the store management. As mentioned earlier, the delivery trucks are sometimes used as temporary storage areas, presumably when the store does not have enough floor space to accommodate the new merchandise. These conditions could be detected and appropriate action taken to rectify them with the system described here.

A second means of improving the organization's management information system is to computerize the maintenance of weekly price data. Currently, this information is entered manually and is error-prone. It would be relatively simple to include this information in the computer data base and make it an integral part of the reports to the buyers.

There is also much room for improvement in the format of the reports given to buyers. At the present time, these are basically data laid out in a systematic tabular format. It is difficult to glean information from these reports by looking at rows and rows of numbers. It would be easier to visualize the dynamics of the demand process with a graphical format — say, k as a function of time and price.

The Control Model: A Summary

The basic inputs to the control model are the coefficients of price and time in the response function for k, the time horizon, and the salvage value of the item. These coefficients could be obtained from regression analysis of current and historical data. They can also be obtained by using the "decision calculus" approach, based on the judgments of the buyers. Successful implementation of this model requires a good infrastructure to capture, store, and maintain transaction data. The model has to be made part of a Decision Support System (DSS) becuase the buyers cannot be expected to spend their time conducting the analysis. The software in the DSS should require a minimum of data manipulation on the part of the buyers (for example, to obtain the coefficients of price and time), allow them to modify any parameters based on their judgment, and give a suggested price path.

The control model could be used as a planning tool to find the point in time at which an item is a candidate for a markdown. It also gives the buyer an idea of the rate of price decrease required to maximize revenues. On the basis of these results and other factors not accounted for in the model, the buyer could plan a markdown schedule at discrete time intervals. Alternatively, if a minimum price reduction is specified, the points in time at which to effect the desired price reduction can be found.

The model can be made sensitive to the size of initial and ending inventory by specifying the salvage value to be a function of the latter. This function (or schedule) is external to the model and can be either based on historical data or upon the judgment of the buyer.

Issues for Further Research

This monograph would not be complete without raising a few interesting questions and problems which require further investigation.

Does a promotion have any carry-over effect? Suppose an item were promoted for one week and then reverted back to its original retail price. Is the sales rate in the weeks following the promotion week any better than it would have been had the item not been promoted? Preliminary evidence from an examination of the plots of k versus time and price indicates that promotions have no carry-over effects. k seems to drop back to the level that would have been expected if there had been no promotion.

Considering the nature of the items — which are basically one-time purchases made by the consumers — this makes sense. That is not to say that promotions serve no purpose: they do draw customers and generate "excitement" in the stores. Promoting a few items could increase the general sales level in a department because of the cross-elasticities. A controlled experiment would give a better insight into the role of promotions for sale of fashion items.

Is a more generalized model needed? The control model developed and solved had only two variables, price and time, in the response function for k (the regression equation). A more generalized model would consider other variables such as inventory and seasonal effects. A nonlinear response function for k may not be easily solvable, and numerical methods may have to be used. These factors would undoubtedly make the model quite complex; and it is not clear if the complexity is worth the effort in terms of improving the end result. The feasibility of using discrete time models — such as dynamic programming — can be explored. The advantage of these models is in their capacity to handle complicated response functions.

Can the success or failure of an item in the Christmas season be predicted? It would be nice to find an early indicator that could predict this. One possibility is to see if the success or failure in the Christmas season has any relationship to the time at which the Christmas season starts influencing the demand for an item, i.e., the point at which k switches from a decreasing to an increasing function over time.

Is it possible to find a clear-cut reorder policy for fashion items? This is closely related to the problem of predicting the failure or success of an item in the Christmas season.

Appendix

Plots of k versus Time and Price by Item

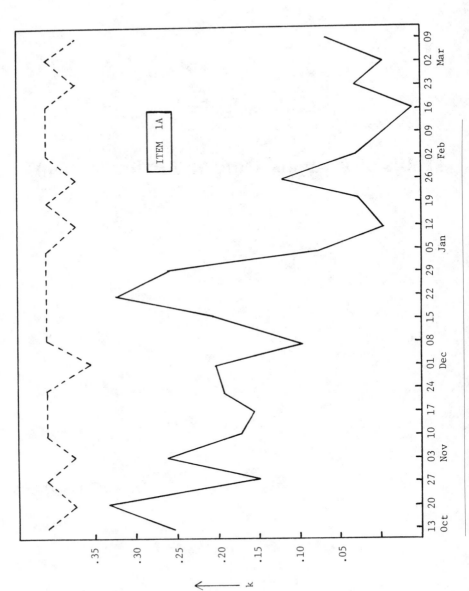

The Variation in Price Is Shown by Dashed Lines at the Top (for all charts in this section).

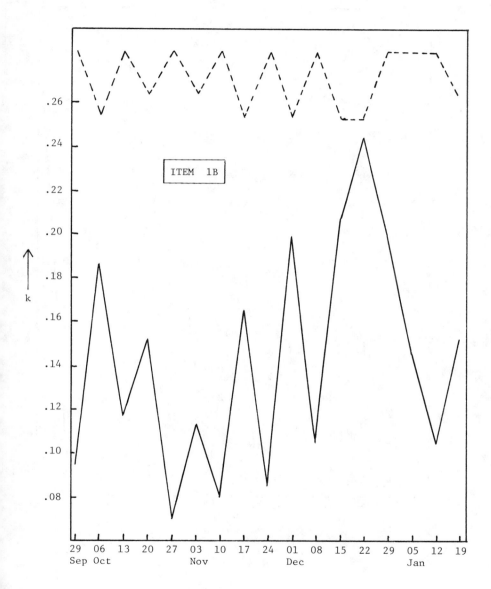

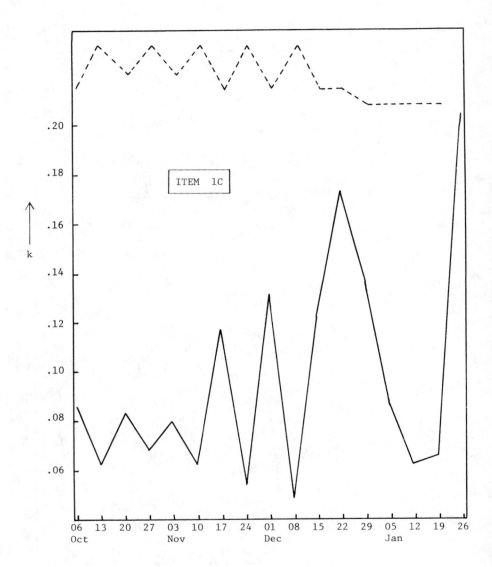

ITEM 1C

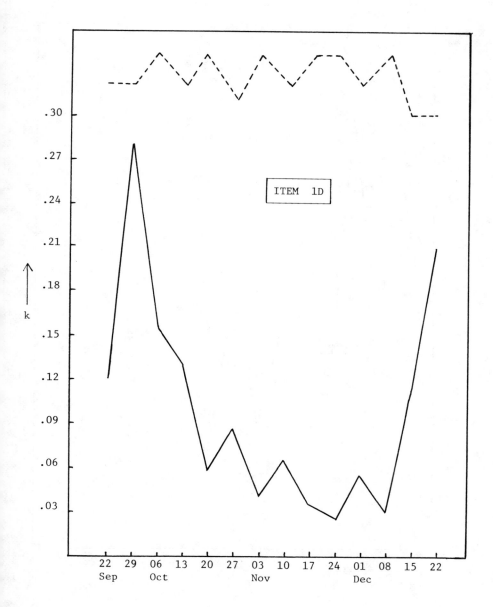

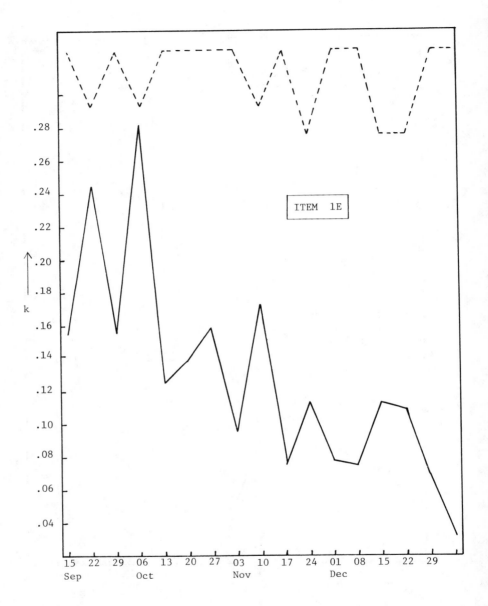

ITEM 1E

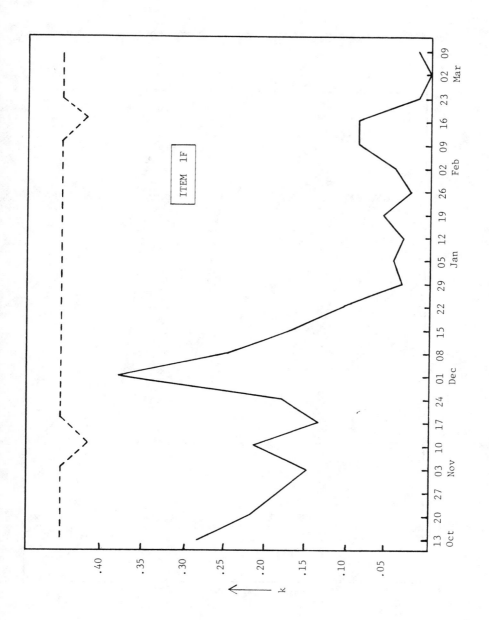

ITEM 1F

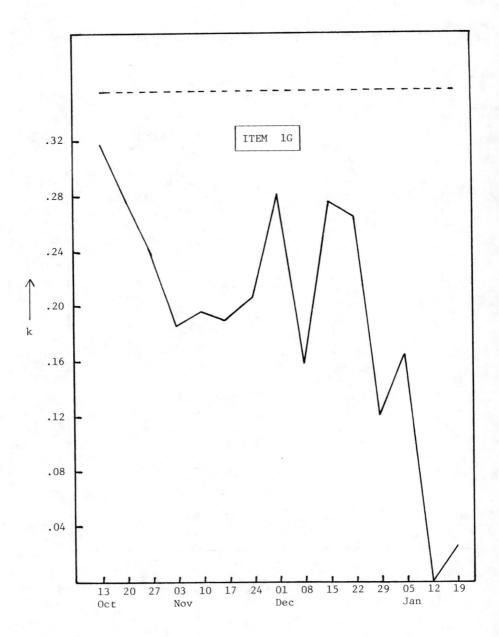

ITEM 1G

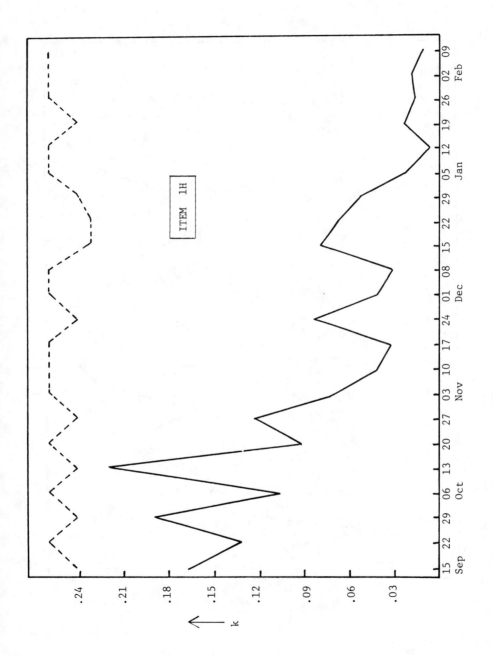

ITEM 1H

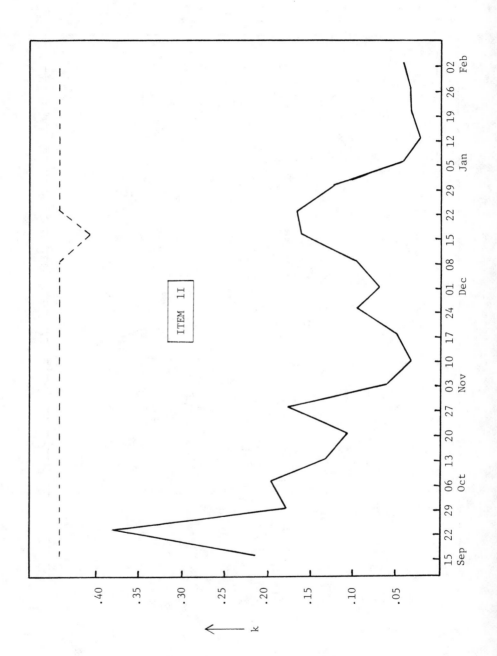

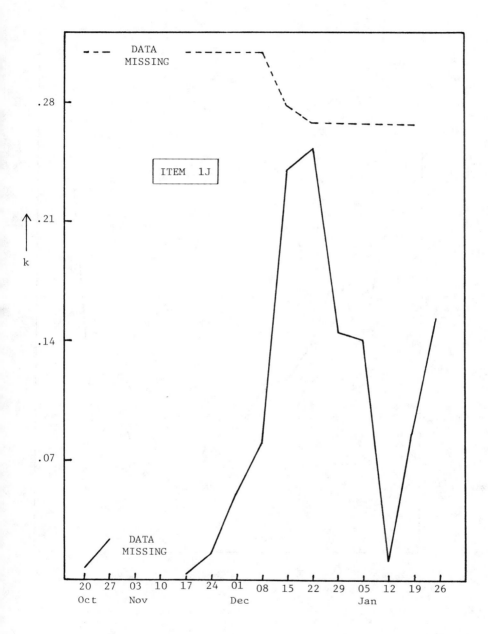

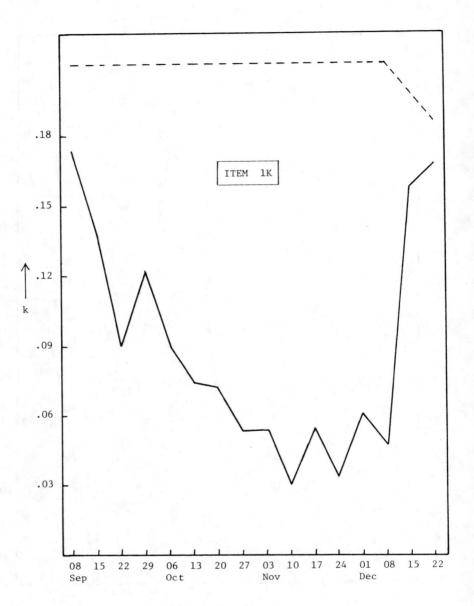

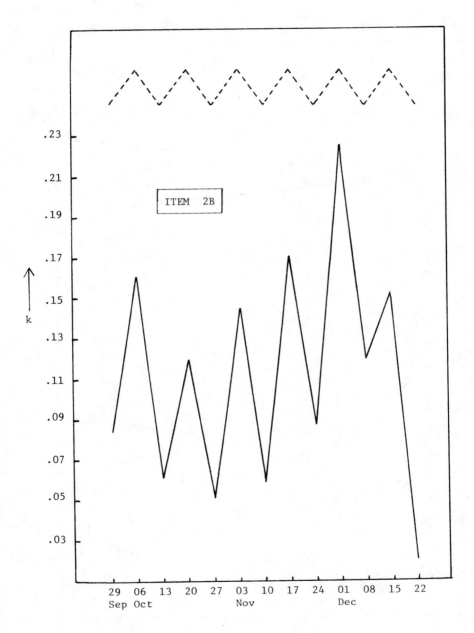

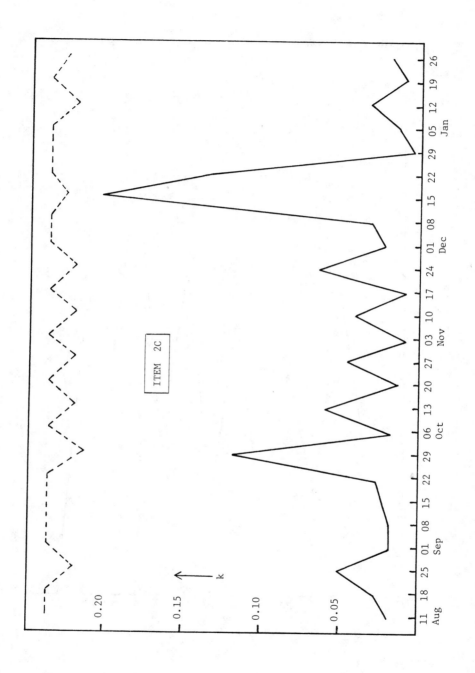

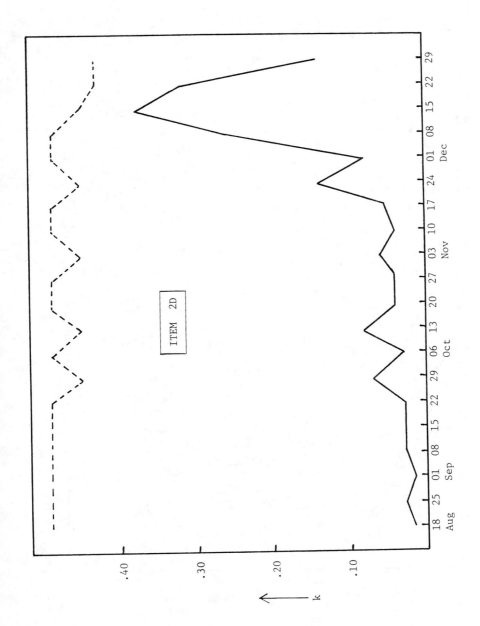

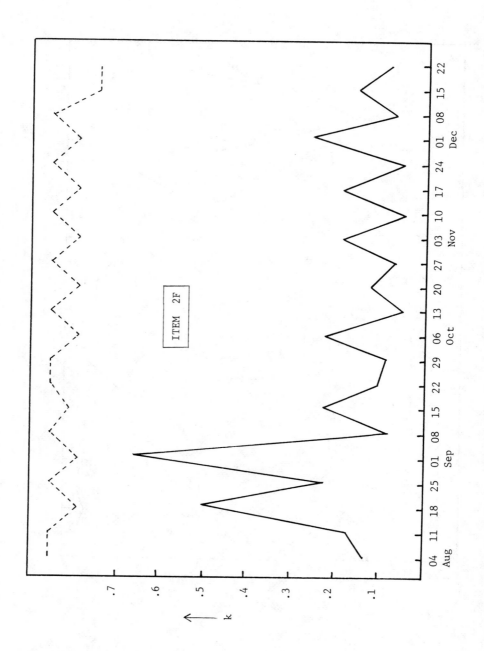

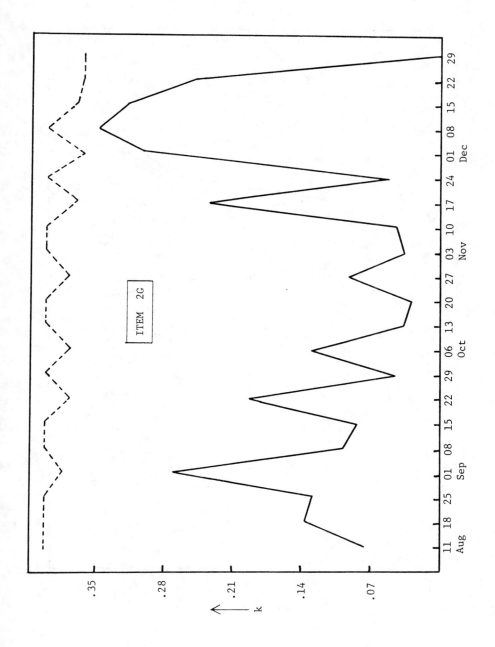

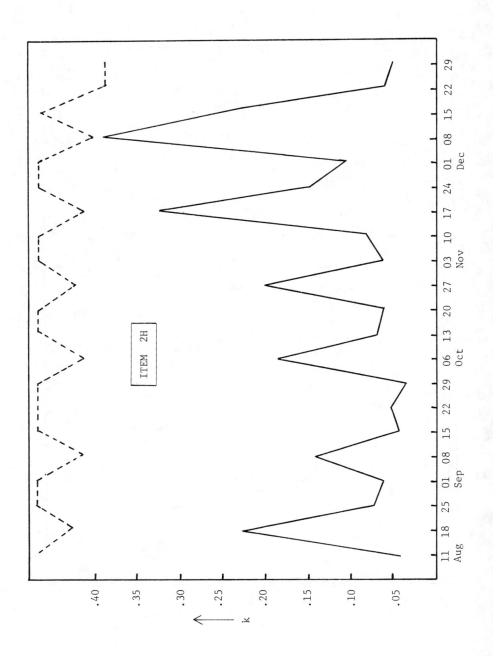

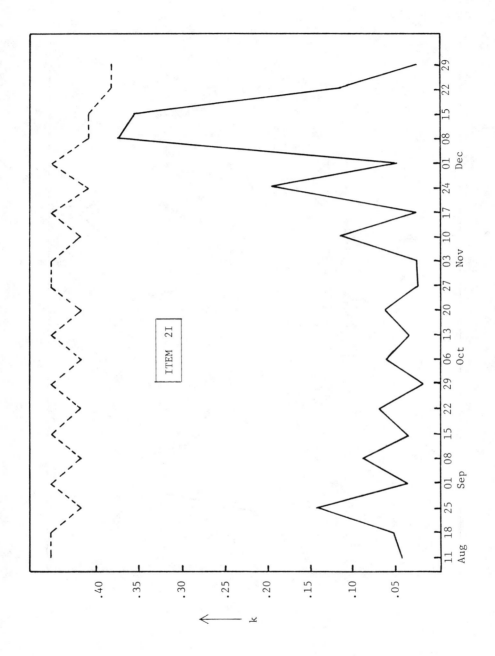

ITEM 2I

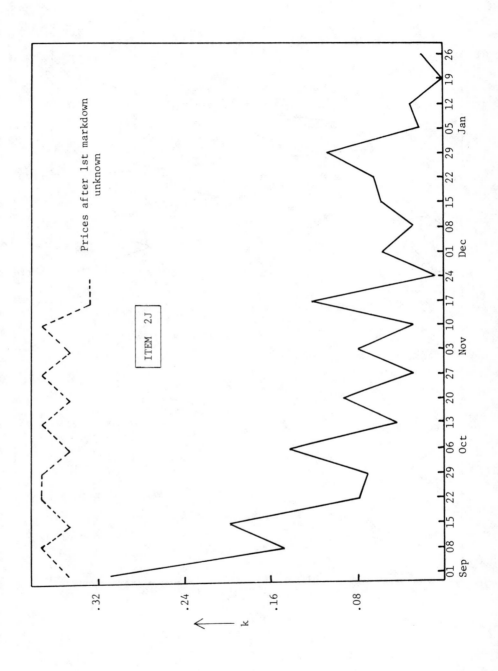

Prices after 1st markdown
unknown

ITEM 2J

k

.32

.24

.16

.08

01 08 15 22 29 06 13 20 27 03 10 17 24 01 08 15 22 29 05 12 19 26
Sep   Oct   Nov   Dec   Jan

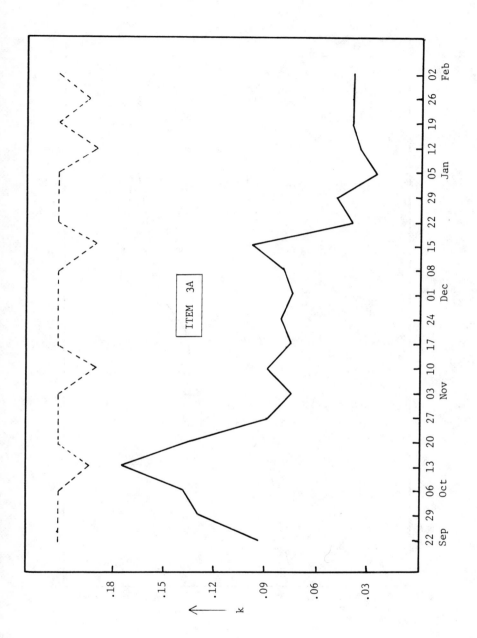

ITEM 3A

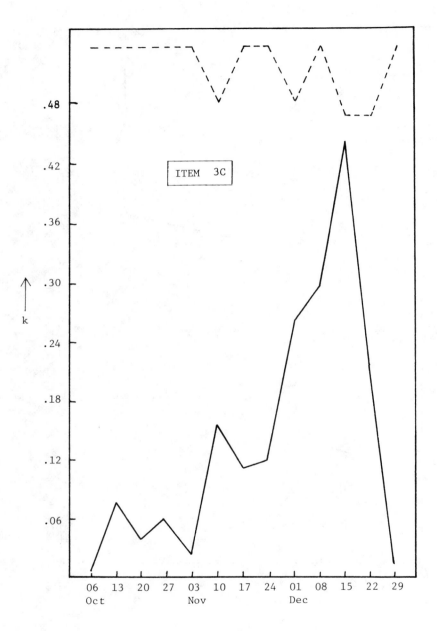

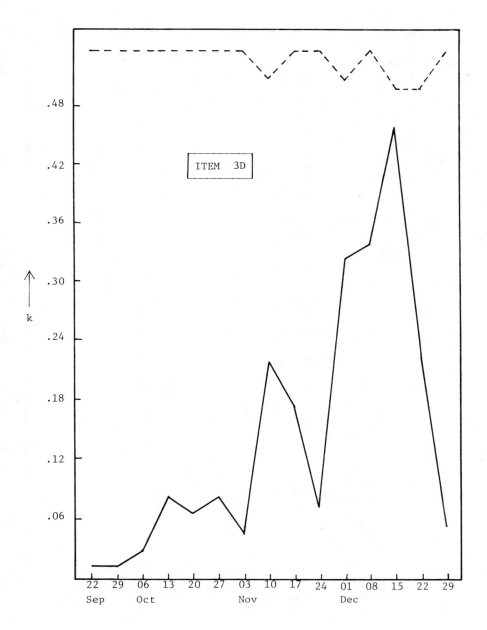

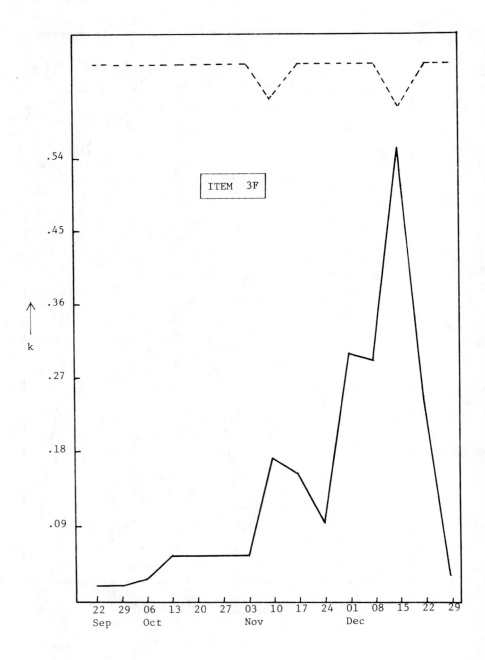

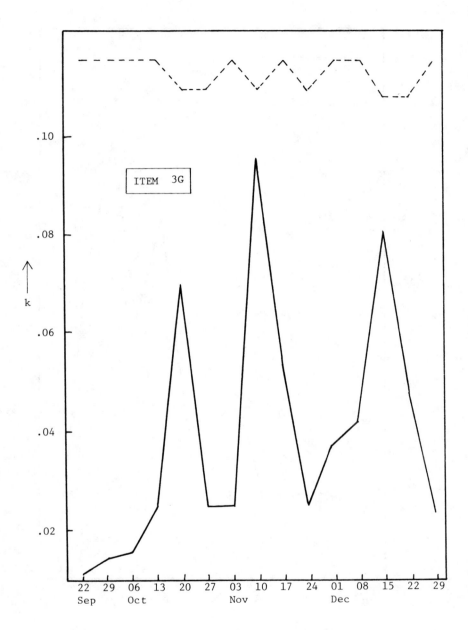

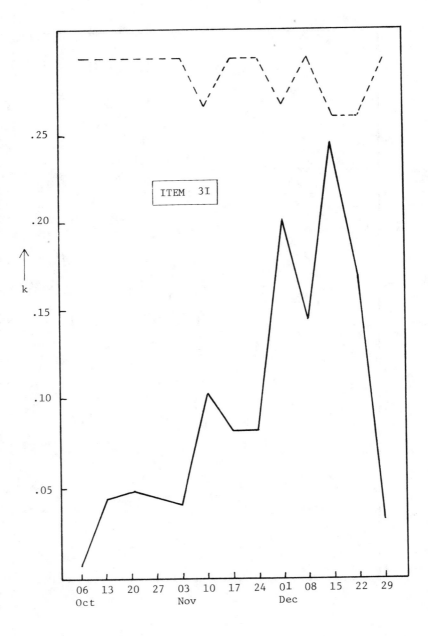

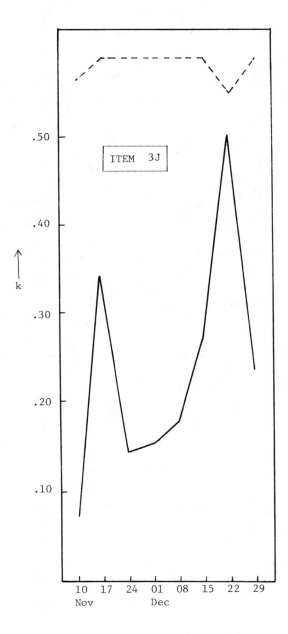

Bibliography

(1) Barankin, E.W., and Denny, J. "Examination of an Inventory Model Incorporating Prob-abilities of Obsolescence," *Logistics Review and Military Logistics Journal* 1(1), 11-25 (1965).

(2) Bellman, R., Glicksberg, I. and Gross, O. "On the Optimal Inventory Equation," *Management Science* 2(1), 83-104 (1955).

(3) Bhat, R.R., and Bucklin, L.P. "Demand Theory for Fashion Merchandise at Retail," Working Paper, School of Business Administration, UC Berkeley (1984).

(4) Braun, M. *Differential Equations and Their Applications.* Springer-Verlag: Berlin (1975).

(5) Brown, W., Lu, J.Y., and Wolfson, R.J. "Dynamic Modeling of Inventories Subject to Obsolescence," *Management Science* 11(1), 51-63, (Sept. 1964).

(6) Bucklin, L.P. "Patterns of Productivity Change Among Traditional Department Stores in the United States," Paper presented at the Symposium on Current Trends in Distribution Research. Brussels (May 1982).

(7) Carlson, P.G., and Tully, J.E. "Fashion Wear Buying: An Economic Approach." *Retail Control* 48-49 (Aug. 1977).

(8) Carlson, P.G., and Tully, J.E. "The Financial Impact of Fashion Wear Markdown Policy." *Retail Control* 48-63 (Jan. 1979).

(9) Cooper, P. "Subjective Economics: Factors in a Psychology of Spending." *Pricing Strategy.* Edited by Bernard Taylor and Gordon Wills, 112-21. Staples: London (1969).

(10) Cyert, R.M., March, J.G. and Moore, C.G. "A Model of Retail Ordering and Pricing by a Department Store." *Quantitative Techniques in Marketing Analysis,* by Frank, Kuehn and Massey, 502-22. Irwin (1962).

(11) Dalrymple, D.J. and Thompson, D.L. *Retailing — An Economic Perspective.* Free Press: New York (1969).

(12) Davidowitz, H.L. "Some of the Capabilities and Impact of Point-of-Sale Devices in the Retail Environment." *Retail Control* 33-43 (Dec. 1972).

(13) Flannel, S. "Departmental Merchandising and Operating Results of 1962." New York: National Retail Merchants Association (1963).

(14) Gross, W.W. "Inventory Management Principles to Help Determine When, What and How Much To Buy." *Retail Control* 20-27 (Feb. 1974).

(15) Hadley, G., and Whitin, T.M. *Analysis of Inventory Systems.* Prentice-Hall: Englewood Cliffs, N.J. (1963).

(16) Hartung, P.H. "A Simple Style Goods Inventory Model." *Management Science* 19 (12), 1452-58 (Aug. 1973).

(17) Hertz, D.B. and Schaffir, K.H. "A Forecasting Method for Management of Seasonal Style-Goods Inventories." *Operations Research* VIII (1), 45-52 (Jan.-Feb. 1960).

(18) IBM Data Processing Application. "IMPACT." 2nd Edition (1967).

(19) Johnson, M. "An Optimization Approach to Display Space Allocation and Product Assortment in Self Service Retail Stores." Working Paper #CP434. Center for Research in Management, UC Berkeley.

(20) Leeds, H.A. "Management Has the Information to Improve Return-on-Inventory Investment." *Retail Control* 34-42 (Nov. 1976).

(21) Lewis, H.W. "Merchandising Fashion in Chain Operations: In a Department Chain Store." *The Management of Fashion Merchandising — A Symposium.* Edited by Kleeberg, I.C. and Cash, R.P. NRMA: New York (1977).

(22) Little, John D.C. "Models and Managers: The Concept of a Decision Calculus." *Management Science* 18(8) (April 1970).

(23) Lodish, L.M. "Applied Dynamic Pricing and Production Models with Specific Application to Broadcast Spot Pricing." *Journal of Marketing Research* XVII 203-11 (May 1980).

(24) Murphy, G.M. *Ordinary Differential Equations and their Solutions.* D. Van Nostrand Co., Inc.: Princeton, N.J. (1960).

(25) Murray, G.R. Jr. and Silver, E.A. "A Bayesian Analysis of the Style Goods Inventory Problem." *Management Science* 12(11), 785-97 (July 1966).

(26) Nahmais, S. "Perishable Inventory Theory: A Review." Presented at the ORSA/TIMS Meeting in Los Angeles (Nov. 1978).

(27) NRMA. *The Buyer's Manual: a Merchandising Handbook.* New York (1965).

(28) Nystrom, H. *Retail Pricing — An Integrated Economic and Psychological Perspective.* Economic Research Institute at the Stockholm School of Economics: Stockholm (1970).

(29) Oxenfeldt, A.R. *Pricing Strategies.* Amacon: New York (1975).

(30) Pessemier, E.A. *Retail Assortments — Some Theoretical and Applied Problems.* Technical Report #80-111. Marketing Science Institute, Research Program (Dec. 1980).

(31) Pierskalla, W.P. "An Inventory Problem with Obsolescence." *Naval Research Logistics Quarterly* 16(2), 217-28 (June 1969).

(32) Rands, T., Vause, R., and Woodward, N. "A Minimal Information Stock Control System for Retail Stores." *Retail Control,* 49-63 (April-May 1974).

(33) Riter, C.B. "The Merchandising Decision Under Uncertainty." *J. of Marketing* 31, 44-47 (Jan. 1967).

(34) Scher, J. "Department Store and Specialty Store Merchandising and Operating Results of 1980" (1981).

(35) Schwartz, B.L. "Optimal Inventory Policies in Perturbed Demand Models." *Management Science* 16(18), 203-11 (April 1980).

(36) Tully, J.E. and Carlson, P.G. "Fashion Wear Buying: An Economic Approach." *Retail Control* 48-57 (Aug. 1977).

(37) Whitin, T.M. "Inventory Control and Price Theory." *Management Science* II(1), 61-68 (Oct. 1955).

(38) Wingate, J.W., and Friedlander, J.S. "The Management of Retail Buying." Englewood Cliffs, N.J.: Prentice-Hall (1963).

(39) Wolfe, H.B. "A Model for Control of Style Merchandise." *IMR* (Winter 1968).

(40) Veinott, A.F., Jr. "The Status of Mathematical Inventory Theory." *Management Science* 12(11) (July 1966).

Index

Advertising: increase in role of fashion, 1; and pricing, effect of, 25–26

Assortments: demand for, and price, 1–2; poor knowledge of, 1; and promotion, 4; and sales: inventory ratio (k), 85–87; sales of, and price, 4; seasonal demand for, 1–2, 4

Barankin and Denny model, 15

Bellman, R., cited, 9

Broadcast spot pricing models, 16

Brown, W., model, 14

Buyers, performance evaluation of, and markdown, 27

Buying, fashion. *See* Fashion buying

Buying function, and institutional structure (*see also* Fashion buying): distribution of merchandise, 22, 24; improvements needed, 85, 87; item categorization, 20; lead times, 22; markdowns, 25–27; markups, 22–23; performance monitoring, 23–24; pricing, 25; process of, 22; reorders, 24; season plans, 20–22

Christmas season: and demand, 86; effect on control theory model, 78–79; predictability of effect, 89; and sales: inventory ratio (k), 41, *43–44, 45–47,* 86; variable, in regression models, 52, *53–57*

Cobb-Douglas model, 52–53

Control theory models (for pricing of (F,NP) items), 61–68, 85: calculation of, 67–68; Christmas season, effect on, 78–79; Decision Support System, 79, *83–84,* 88; demonstration of, 71, 73, *74–77;* implementation of, 70–*72,* 79; limitations of, 79–80; price changes, not considered, 79–80; summarized, 88

Cyert model, 1, 12–14

Cyert, R.M., cited, 85

Data collection, 29–36: availability, 29–31; computerized, 23–24; difficulties of, 2–3, 29–31; historical sales data, use of, 29–30; and inventory, 33–34, 46; and markdowns, 31–32, 34; and markups, 32–33; mechanics of, 29–30, 32; need for improvement in, 87; price data, 31; and pricing, 31–33; promotions, 32, 35; reporting errors, 31; returns, 31

Decision Calculus, use in pricing models, 60

Decision Support System (DSS), 79, *83–84,* 88

Demand: decrease of, and time path, 59–61; factors of, and analysis of sales: inventory ratio (k), 37–50; lack of hard data, 5; patterns of (*see also* Inventory models), 8; seasonal, and time paths, 2, 4, 86; variance of, at production and retail levels, 2

Distribution and redistribution of merchandise, 22, 24

Fashion, increase of in softgoods merchandising, 1

Fashion buying (*see also* Buying function): creation of sales assortments, and time paths, 4–5; and increase in markdowns and markups, 1; lack of systematic study, 1

Fashion inventory, management of: data collection, problems of, 2–5; and economic, sociological and psychological factors, 3; production level, 2–3; reasons for holding, 7; retail level, 3; "rules of thumb" and lack of hard-data models, 2, 5; techniques, and technology, 3–4; variance of demand, production and retail, 2

Fashion merchandising: institutional structure, 19–20, 22–27; lack of systematic study, reasons for, 1; and season, 4; and time path of assortments, 1–2, 4–5